Presented To:

_____

Presented By:

_____

Date:

_____

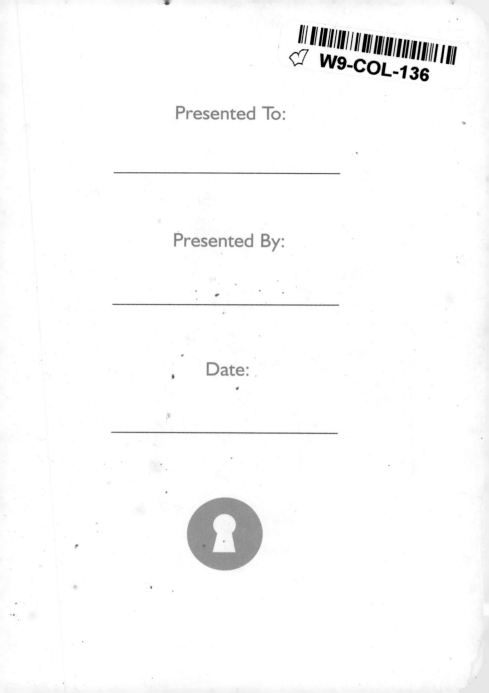

words

to live by

Unlock the POWER of Words to
Change Your Life Forever

words

to live by

Reflections & Insights on the
Most Life–Changing & Thought–
Provoking Words in the Bible

BETHANYHOUSE

Words to Live By
ISBN 0-7642-2923-0

Copyright © 2004 by GRQ, Inc.
Brentwood, Tennessee 37027

Published by Bethany House Publishers
11400 Hampshire Avenue South
Bloomington, Minnesota 55438
www.bethanyhouse.com

Bethany House Publishers is a division of Baker Publishing Group, Grand Rapids, Michigan.

Scripture quotations noted CEV are taken from The Contemporary English Version. © 1991 by the American Bible Society. Used by permission.

Scripture quotations noted KJV are taken from the King James Version.

Scripture quotations noted MKJV are taken from the Modern King James Version of the Holy Bible, Copyright © 1962, 1990, 1993, 1998, 1999. Used by permission of the copyright holder, Jay P. Green, Sr.

Scripture quotations noted NASB are taken from the New American Standard Bible® Copyright © 1960, 1962, 1963–1968, 1971, 1973–1975, 1977, 1995 by the Lockman Foundation. Used by permission.

Scripture quotations noted NIV are taken from the *Holy Bible: New International Version* (North American Edition)®. Copyright © 1973–1978, 1984, by the International Bible Society. Used by permission of Zondervan. All rights reserved.

Scripture quotations noted NKJV are taken from The New King James Version. Copyright © 1979, 1980, 1982, Thomas Nelson, Inc., Publishers.

Scripture quotation noted NLT are taken from the *Holy Bible*, New Living Translation, copyright © 1996. Used by permission of Tyndale House Publishers, Inc., Wheaton, Illinois 60189. All rights reserved.

Scripture quotations noted NRSV are taken from the New Revised Standard Version of the Bible, copyright © 1989 by the Division of Christian Education of the National Council of the Churches of Christ in the USA. Used by permission. All rights reserved.

Library of Congress Control Number 2004010925

Compiler and Editor: Lila Empson
Writer: Stephen Mansfield
Design: Whisner Design Group

04 05 06 / 4 3 2 1

Broadly speaking, the short
words are the best, and
the old words best of all.

Sir Winston Churchill

Contents

Introduction

Christianity is uniquely a religion of words. A person can be a good Muslim, a good Buddhist, and a good Hindu and never read a single word. But Christianity, springing as it does from Jewish soil, requires the mastery of language. In fact, it is hard to communicate the Christian faith without the vocabulary that has come to be associated with it. Try to explain the religion Jesus founded without the words *sin, crucifixion, saved, justified, sanctified,* and *holy*. It is nearly impossible, and it shows how closely faith and language are associated in the Christian faith.

Yet there is more to Christianity than intellectual understanding. Jesus taught his

disciples that God's Spirit lives in the words, telling them in one instance, "The words I have spoken to you are spirit and they are life" (John 6:63 NIV). This is what makes the words so important in Christianity and also why believers are expected to memorize them, speak them, meditate on them, rehearse them, remind each other of them, and search for their deepest meaning.

It is to encourage just such reveling in words that this book is written. Each word herein is explored in such a way as to stir the heart and instruct the mind. It is hoped that from new depths of meaning new power for the soul will spring, for this is, after all, the way of the Christian faith.

This is what we speak, not in words taught by human wisdom but in words taught by the Spirit, expressing spiritual truths in spiritual words.

🔒

1 Corinthians 2:13 NIV

The Life You Were Made For

a·bun·dance, noun.

1. a great plenty.
2. an overflowing supply.
3. a provision beyond mere need.
4. **Biblical:** a bounty beyond expectation and merit.
5. **Personal:** the kind of meaningful, prosperous life God wants for you.

a · bun · dance

Humankind has loved a certain kind of story throughout its history. This tale is found in the literature and mythology of almost every culture. It goes something like this: A young man is known to be good and true. He is a peasant and he does his work well, is kind to others, and lives his simple life with joy. Then one day he is told that he is the long lost son of a king. He is taken to the king's castle, where the young man grows into a noble ruler himself. And the land prospers. The people of his old village say that they always knew the young man was special.

> The thief does not come except to steal and to kill and destroy. I have come so that they might have life, and that they might have it more abundantly.
>
> John 10:10 MKJV

You may love these stories, love the idea of a Cinderella, of a pauper who becomes a prince, of a commoner who is royal after all. You may love the stories because, somewhere deep inside, you sense that you are made for more than you have ever known. You have some inner

words
to live by

belief that the life you are living is far beneath what you were designed for, and you find in these stories a match to the yearning of your heart.

The truth is, your heart is right. You are made for more. You were made for intimacy with the Creator of the universe. Your soul is hard-wired for abundance, for blessing, for love, for grace, and for holy community. This is what you hunger for, whether you know it or not. It is what the eternity in your heart points you to, even subconsciously.

But then you live in this world, and this world presses its message on your heart. With every wound, every sin, and every disappointment the message is, "Live small. Just survive. This life isn't made for happiness." So you absorb these arrows into your heart and live in The Land of the Small the rest of your days.

Jesus came to call you out of The Land of the Small. He came to restore you to your true self. He took the lack and the wounds and the sins that separate you from your greater life and he destroyed them on his cross. Then he turned to you and said, "I've come to give you an abundant life." The word *abundant* in Greek means "something above the ordinary." Jesus appealed to that eternity in the human heart and said, in essence, "I've come to give you the life your heart has been telling you is yours. I've come to make you who you really are: a possessor of an abundant life."

> The abundant life is one in which every promise of God has been answered with a resounding "yes" of experience.
> **CHRISTOPHER SYNN**

eless grace mercy love faith goodness truth freedom hope
orgiveness peace humble holiness obey repent perfect submit
serve fellowship comforter transformed noble character church

If, by the trespass
of the one man,
death reigned
through that one
man, how much
more will those
who receive God's
abundant provision
of grace and of the
gift of righteous-
ness reign in life
through the one
man, Jesus Christ.
Romans 5:17 NIV

Paul understood this. He constantly chided the believers he taught for living beneath the life Jesus had come to give them. He knew they were overcomers, shining ones, heirs of the good gifts of God. In fact, when Paul's churches misbehaved and he searched for some phrase to describe their behavior, he settled on "mere men." In other words, the worst thing Paul could think of to call Christians who had compromised themselves was that they were merely human, merely existing. They had slipped beneath the glory Jesus had given them and designed them for.

The key to the abundant life is found in something Paul told the Ephesians. He told them that there is a power in the believer that is capable of doing far more than human beings can ask or imagine. This is the dream of the human heart restored. Ask for it, take it for your own, refuse to live with anything less.

words
to live by

Things you probably didn't know about *abundance:*

❶ One of the words for abundance in the Greek New Testament is *hyperbole.* The English word of the same spelling is derived from it and it means, literally, "to throw far beyond."

❶ When the English Pilgrims sailed to the New World, one of their number wrote that they dreamed of making their new home "a land of the abundant life for all nations."

If I were asked to state the great objective which Church and State are both demanding for the sake of every man and woman and child in this country, I would say that that great objective is "a more abundant life."
FRANKLIN DELANO ROOSEVELT

The abundant life is far more than material prosperity. It is the life of a heart fulfilled.
HAROLD PAUL

Now to him who is able to do exceeding abundantly above all that we ask or think, according to the power that works in us, to Him be glory in the church and by Christ Jesus throughout all ages, forever.
Ephesians 3:20–21 MKJV

God, I have settled for the small when you have called me to the abundant. Forgive me, heal me, and grant me the abundant life Jesus came to give. Make me a trophy of your grace. To your glory.
—Amen.

a · b u n · d a n c e

The Dark Mask of Hurt

an·ger, noun.

1. an emotional excitement caused by intense displeasure.
2. a passionate emotional response to injury.
3. an intense feeling of the soul in the face of injustice and cruelty.
4. **Biblical:** a strong emotional agitation that must be mastered.
5. **Personal:** your soul's negative response to pain.

a n · g e r

Two Greek words are used for anger in the New Testament. The first is *thumos*. This is the healthier version, the kind of anger that is part of just being alive. It means "the soul's response to pain, suffering, and injustice." It tends to be more seasonal, is usually tied to wrongdoing, and it ends when the condition that created it ends.

> Man's anger does not bring about the righteous life that God desires.
> James 1:20 NIV

This version of anger is common to the human experience. In fact, a great deal of good comes from it. This is the anger that moves a mother to discipline a child or a man to correct his friend's behavior. It is the anger that moves a woman to write a letter to a member of congress or work to right a social wrong. When Paul told believers to be angry but without sin, he meant this version of anger, the kind that can be good if handled well.

words
to live by

The second Greek word for anger in the New Testament is the dangerous one. It is *orge.* It means more than just the feeling of anger. It describes what happens when unanswered anger is allowed to seep into the soul, into the innermost heart, and build a fortress there. Wrongs are turned over and over in the mind. The words of pain and protest are rehearsed aloud. Revenge is planned. The heart hardens and rage is seldom far away. This is *orge*, and it is a killer.

In fact, it may be a killer in the most literal sense. The English word for anger comes from the Latin word that means to choke or strangle. The word has long been used to describe something that is narrow, strained, or drawn together. Indeed, the word *angina* comes from it. It means the pain that comes from a tightening of the arteries, and you have to wonder if a connection doesn't exist between the heart problems in this generation and the intense anger so many carry inside.

Even if it doesn't kill, this *orge* kind of anger makes the human heart narrow, like the word suggests. It diminishes. You live out of your lesser self. You find that your capacity for love and the forgiveness that makes love possible is squelched. You grow hard, unfeeling, and alone. You are locked in the prison of anger.

Anger is a
short madness.
HORACE

But there is hope. Anger has a secret to tell that

The Dark Mask of Hurt

Be angry, and yet do not sin; do not let the sun go down on your anger.

Ephesians 4:26 NASB

may help you break its hold and free you to live large again. It is this: Anger is most often a mask for hurt. Usually, people respond in anger when they feel emotional pain, to keep them from having to delve deeply into what has hurt them. Anger is easier. Anger is external, about someone else, and has a wonderful power to turn the gaze from the real issue: hurt. In fact, it is often a lifetime of unexamined hurt masked with anger that makes the kind of raging, bitter person you strive to avoid and hope not to become.

You might become a bitter person, though, unless you learn that that the soft underbelly of anger is hurt and that a hurt tended—forgiven, cleansed, understood, and outlived—is the fresh spring water that douses anger's fire.

❶

Dare to examine the pain at the heart of your anger. It will take courage. You may have to examine ugly patterns in your life to get at the source of that anger in your history. Then you can "own the hurt," see it healed, and destroy the fortress that "orge" has built in your heart.

words
to live by

Things you probably didn't know about *anger:*

❶ Increasingly, doctors are understanding the connection between emotions and illness. Among all that a human being can feel, anger is connected to more sicknesses and physical deformities than any other single emotion.

❶ It could be argued that people are angrier today than ever before in history and that this is producing a public health risk. The fact is, anger is increasing so drastically as a factor in society that it is becoming a leading safety factor, giving rise to such concerns as "road rage," "air rage," and "sports rage."

Anger is a weed; hate is the tree.
SAINT AUGUSTINE

Pride was not made for men, nor furious anger for them that are born of a woman.
THE APOCRYPHA

I knew that You are a gracious God, and merciful, slow to anger, and of great kindness, and One who repents over calamity.
Jonah 4:2 MKJV

God, forgive me for the sinful anger in my life. Give me the courage to face my wounds, forgive those who have hurt me, and live free of the destructive anger than has been in my life. I ask it in your name.
—Amen.

a n · g e r

ess grace mercy love faith goodness truth freedom hope
orgiveness peace humble holiness obey repent perfect submit
serve fellowship comforter transformed noble character church

The Power of the Godly Life

a·noint·ing, noun.

1. an application of power or the symbols of power.
2. the presence of God's Spirit.
3. a choosing and endowment for service.
4. *Biblical:* a flow of power for a specified purpose.
5. *Personal:* the power of God to live the life you are called to.

a · n o i n t · i n g

God is not a harsh taskmaster. He is not like the domineering coach or the critical parent or the angry boss. He doesn't require more than you can do and then condemn you for not doing it. God has set his standards high, but then he has made sure you have what you need to reach those standards.

You have an anointing from the Holy One.

I John 2:20 MKJV

Part of the provision he has made is what the Bible calls "the anointing." The word *anointing* means "a flow of grace and power to achieve a desired result." Sometimes the word refers simply to the smearing of oil because this was the outward sign of an anointing in the ancient world. But more often the word means this flow of power God has given you to help you achieve what he has called you to do.

words
to live by

Normally, people think of the anointed as those who are uniquely gifted. They have no problem seeing their pastor as anointed, nor is it hard for them to see an "anointing" on a famous Christian musician or on a gifted Christian writer. But it may be hard for you to believe that you can be anointed. Yet this is just what Scripture states. Believers have an anointing from Jesus. It is a deposit of God's Spirit that is given to you to help you live the Christian life and to replicate the nature of Jesus in you. This is why, when Jesus first saw his disciples after his resurrection, he breathed on them and said, "Receive the Holy Spirit." It is also why 1 John tells you that you know you have Jesus living in you by the Spirit he has given you.

Clearly, to be born again is to have what the Bible calls an anointing, a gift of the Holy Spirit to help you be what you are supposed to be. God has not called you to do what he has not given you the power to accomplish. He has given you his spirit, which Ephesians 3 says is "able to do beyond all you can ask or imagine." This Spirit is "at work" in you and is accomplishing God's purposes every moment.

Not all the water in the rough rude sea can wash the balm from an anointed King.
WILLIAM SHAKESPEARE

uness grace mercy love faith goodness truth freedom hope
orgiveness peace humble holiness obey repent perfect submit
serve fellowship comforter transformed noble character church

The Power of the Godly Life

> God, your God,
> has set you above
> your companions
> by anointing you
> with the oil of joy.
> **Hebrews 1:9** NIV

This is why some of the hardest things for a Christian to do are simply called "fruits of the Spirit" by God. You don't have to manufacture them. You simply have to let the Spirit grow them in your life. It is hard, after all, to love the unlovely, to be patient when you aren't feeling it, and to lay down your life for others. These don't come naturally, and they don't come by human effort. Yet they are clearly what God desires. Thankfully, you have an anointing from God, a flow of grace and power, specifically sent to help you fulfill the will of God—for your soul, for the church, and in the world.

🔒

Take inventory for a moment and find the places in your life where you are striving hard to change or produce fruit. Understand that God has already made the provision you need. You are already anointed to be what you are called to be. Repent of your striving, ask God for the flow of his anointing, and let the power you need fill your life.

words
to live by

etcetera . . .

Things you might not know about *anointing:*

❶ In Isaiah 20:27, the older translations say that "the anointing will break the yoke," but the original word translated *anointing* is really *fat*. The idea is, the animal will grow so big and fat that he will break the yoke. The word *anointing* was used, though, because anointing oil was made from fat.

❶ The word for anointing, *charisma*, is a compound word: *icharis*, meaning power, plus the suffix *ma*, meaning "toward a goal." One scholar has suggested that the word might be translated "power flow."

It is the common deed accomplished while the common man is under God's anointing that thrills the angels.
DWIGHT MOODY

The anointing is not the possession of preachers but the liberation of the laity.
DEREK PRINCE

How God anointed Jesus of Nazareth with the Holy Spirit and power, and how he went around doing good and healing all who were under the power of the devil, because God was with him.
Acts 10:38 NIV

God, forgive me for straining in the flesh to accomplish what your Spirit was sent to do. Thank you for anointing, that flow of grace and power sent to achieve your will in my life. Let me walk in it and be pleasing in your sight through it.
—Amen.

a · n o i n t · i n g

ness grace mercy love faith goodness truth freedom hope
orgiveness peace humble holiness obey repent perfect submit
serve fellowship comforter transformed noble character church

beau·ty, noun.

1. that which gives pleasure to the senses.
2. that which pleasurably exalts the mind or the spirit.
3. a particular grace, feature, or ornament.
4. **Biblical:** a characteristic of God that is reflected in his creation.
5. **Personal:** what you esteem in God, appreciate in his creation, and seek to become.

beau·ty

The Other Language of God

The devil led him up to a high place and showed him in an instant all the kingdoms of the world. And he said to him, "I will give you all their authority and splendor, for it has been given to me and I can give it to anyone I want to."
Luke 4:5–6 NIV

Life today is fast paced, and getting close to nature is getting close to God. No, nature isn't God, but nature is a revelation of God. Often, when people talk about getting "back to nature" they are speaking from the soul's need for communion with the divine. Nature, beauty, the glory of creation—all are revelations of God.

People often think that what they see in the natural world is just basic nature, the way creation has to be. But this isn't so. When God made the world, he made everything in it to speak of him, to reveal himself to humankind. God has so revealed himself in the natural world that Romans 1 says the atheist is without excuse for not believing in God. The reason? "What may be known about God is plain to them." How? "For since the cre-

words
to live by

ation of the world God's invisible qualities—his eternal power and divine nature—have been clearly seen, being understood from what has been made, so that men are without excuse." God has so revealed himself in nature that humankind should believe in him on the basis of that revelation alone.

This is why you are drawn to the beauty of the world around you. It is God's beauty, and your soul was designed to behold it and be changed by it. Example: You step outside into the chill air on a starry evening and gaze above while holding a loved one. It is a touching moment. And it is also a divine moment. Those starry skies you stare at with such wonder are a language God uses to speak to you. Remember Psalm 19:1–2: "The heavens declare the glory of God; the skies proclaim the work of his hands. Day after day they pour forth speech; night after night they display knowledge" (NIV).

Or perhaps you love the sea and the wonder of ships on the waves. You watch the undulating waters and the glory of the sea creatures. Everything you see is feeding you inwardly, reaching in some unspoken way to your core. Why? Because the sea is a revelation of God. As Psalm 107:23 says, "They that go down to the sea in ships, that do business in great waters; these see the works of the Lord, and his wonders in the deep" (KJV).

O world, as God has made it! All is beauty.
ROBERT BROWNING

unless grace mercy love faith goodness truth freedom hope
orgiveness peace humble holiness obey repent perfect submit
serve fellowship comforter transformed noble character church

The Other Language of God

> The Lord God
> made all kinds of
> trees grow out of
> the ground—trees
> that were pleasing
> to the eye and
> good for food.
> **Genesis 2:9** NIV

It is this way with everything that is made. The button nose of a baby, the refreshment of a cool breeze, the way snow graces the ground, the wonder of fire, the majesty of hills, the thrill of trees reaching to heaven. These aren't just nature's accidents. These were designed by God to speak to you. It is no wonder that you reach to the beautiful, no wonder that art has replaced sports as the metaphor in this present age. Humans are in desperate need of beauty, surrounded as they are by the garish and the bland.

The challenge for you is twofold. First, you must not let your modern pace and techno-focus talk you out of the need for beauty. If you have to be reminded to stop and smell the roses, you are already far behind. You don't need a two-minute flower break. You need to position yourself so your soul can drink in. You must revel in nature, art, people, and sensation as much as God allows.

🔒

The answer to your soul's cry for nature is to experience beauty as a language. Why did God design the world as he has? What does a tree "say"? No, it will not speak words, but it does speak symbols of God. What are they? Meditating on these questions will change your experience of nature and allow you to hear the message of God your soul yearns for.

words
to live by

Things you might not know about *beauty:*

0 A principle has long been confirmed by experts in theology, psychology, and history. It is this: human beings become what they behold. Behold beauty, and the soul flourishes. Behold the ugly and dark, and life becomes the same.

0 A California computer firm became so concerned about the "techno-focus" of its employees that it began to require a ten-minute "beauty break" every day. Workers were required to admire something nontechnical in a film, a book, or outdoors for those ten minutes. What happened? Happier workers and greater productivity. What else?

Beauty is God's handwriting.
CHARLES KINGSLEY

He has made everything beautiful in its time.
Ecclesiastes 3:11 KJV

Beauty is truth, truth beauty—that is all ye know on earth, and all ye need to know.
JOHN KEATS

God, you have made all things beautiful to express the beauty in you. Let me know you through what you have made and love you for what is revealed.
—Amen.

beau·ty

car·nal, *adjective.*

1. pertaining to the flesh.
2. issuing from crude bodily pleasures and appetites.
3. having a physical rather than an intellectual or spiritual orientation.
4. **Biblical:** governed by unredeemed human nature and animal desires.
5. **Personal:** ruled by your body and a lust for the impure.

car·nal

> Those who live according to the sinful nature have their minds set on what that nature desires; but those who live in accordance with the Spirit have their minds set on what the Spirit desires.
>
> **Romans 8:5** NIV

God made Adam and Eve perfect. They were without sin or imperfection. They enjoyed an unhindered relationship with God, they ruled over creation, and they delighted in each other. They were the perfect creatures of a perfect paradise.

Then it came. "God is holding out on you," the devil told them. "He knows that if you eat the forbidden fruit you will be as gods. He's trying to keep you down, to keep the good stuff from you." So Adam and Eve disobeyed God, were thrown out of their paradise, and fell.

They fell. What does that mean? It means they were cut off from God, yes, but it also means that something changed inside them. Some have suggested that their spirits fell into their souls, but this

words
to live by

cannot be known with certainty. What can be known is that they and their descendants became increasingly ruled by the cravings of their bodies and their lesser natures. Whereas once they had been noble, spiritual creatures, living in fellowship with God and doing his will almost effortlessly, now they had descended into some kind of slavery to the dark side of themselves.

The Bible calls this condition "carnal." It means "governed by the fleshy, lusty, lower appetites." Literally, it means "meat oriented," meaning drawn from the body and the drives that are centered in the body. It is a kind of prison, for while human beings are certainly meant to have physical drives and even enjoy them, they are not meant to be governed by them or to be ruled by the destructive side of them.

When Adam and Eve fell, all humankind fell with them. And now all people live in a culture built on carnality. In fact, human society seems to feed the carnal side of the soul more than ever in history. Look around. If the culture isn't pushing food, it's pushing sex. If it isn't pushing sex, it's pushing vanity. If it isn't pushing vanity, it's pushing pride of ownership. Each of these carnal drives is fed by a constant stream of media, carefully crafted to strengthen the lesser drives and send people out in search of fulfillment.

> When I am carnal, I am a meathead. That's what the word means, "meaty, fleshy, from the flesh." I don't want to be a meathead anymore.
> **KENNETH COPELAND**

Living From the Lesser Self

You are still carnal.
For where there
are envy, strife, and
divisions among
you, are you not
carnal and behaving
like mere men?
I Corinthians 3:3
NKJV

That is why you have to fight for the spiritual life like never before. The carnal is killing you, robbing you of everything from peace to prosperity. You must soar above it. You must feed the inner being, what Paul calls the invisible "man of the heart," with the word of God, with prayer, with pure conversations, and with a holiness of life. You are going to have to cut off the "feeder systems" of your carnal nature. You can enjoy movies but not the ones that encourage you in the very deeds God forbids. You can enjoy food, clothes, fun, and romance, but all within God's boundaries and without the idolatrous focus that the present culture encourages. After all, Jonah 2:8 says that "those who cling to worthless idols forfeit the grace that could be theirs" (NIV).

The Christian is in a battle for the spiritual as against the carnal. All of his culture is against him. This is why you must feed your soul on the Word of God, meditate on the noble and the pure, and do everything in your power to strengthen the spiritual being you really are. And pray, so that God will give you grace to live above the carnal and the low.

words
to live by

Things you might not know about *carnal:*

A famous philosopher and man of letters was recently asked which element of modern culture most distinguished it from other cultures throughout history. He said, "catering to the carnal life as man once catered to the divine."

Psychologists have identified a "law of diminishing sensation." It means that every pleasure people pursue gradually becomes less pleasing so they have to give themselves to it more and more to achieve the same level of gratification. This is the basis of addiction.

God, my carnality is keeping me from you. Turn to me anyway.
SAINT AUGUSTINE

A carnal church is a church which has nothing to offer the world for it is a product of the world.
CHRISTOPHER SYNN

The carnal mind is enmity against God; for it is not subject to the law of God, nor indeed can be.
Romans 8:7 NKJV

God, you have made me to soar in your Spirit, but I have often chosen to live in my lesser, carnal self. Forgive me and grant me the grace to sow to the spiritual so I might reap a spiritual harvest.
—Amen.

car·nal

The Price of Glory

char·ac·ter, noun.

1. the features that distinguish a man or a woman from his or her peers.
2. the good qualities that are esteemed and respected in a person.
3. the attributes that make a person valuable to society.
4. *Biblical:* the fruit of hardship approached in faith.
5. *Personal:* what God etches in your life through suffering.

c h a r · a c · t e r

Not only this, but we also exult in our tribulations, knowing that tribulation brings about perseverance; and perseverance, proven character; and proven character, hope.

Romans 5:3–4 NASB

The two political candidates debated heatedly as the eager crowd looked on. Each man running for office spoke his mind, sometimes moving the onlookers to excited applause and sometimes falling flat to almost embarrassing silence. Each one stood his ground, made his argument, and fought his opponent as though to the death. In the back of the room stood an aged writer. Stroking his white beard, he thought deeply about each man and, when asked what he thought, said, "One wishes that they had both suffered more."

This writer wanted to see character in the two candidates. He wanted to see the attributes of the great man, the weightiness of thought and deed that distinguishes leaders from the pack. And he knew that this kind of character comes from hardship, from the suffering that

words
to live by

etches grace and wisdom into the life of those who endure in faith.

What the writer knew is one of the most difficult of Christian teachings: that God uses suffering and hardship to shape human beings in his image and make them useful in his hands. For those who are lost and without God in the world, suffering happens but it has no meaning, no promise of a good result. For those whose trust is in God, though, suffering is hard but redemptive. God uses suffering to wean believers from immaturity, and suffering breaks the power of the world from their lives, moves them to desperation for Jesus, and fashions them for their destiny.

Once you understand this, you see the life you hope to live in a different light. Perhaps you dream of a life of leadership and greatness, like that of Winston Churchill. But do you know the suffering that made the man?

Churchill grew up a sickly stutterer whose father truly hated him, and young Churchill never did well in school. He suffered depressions all his life so that even when he was prime minister of England he wouldn't stay in a room with a balcony for fear he might throw himself off. One of his daughters died in infancy, another committed suicide, and he was estranged from his son for years at a time. He was for long periods the most vilified man in England and lost more elections than any other politician of his age. This was the life of Winston Churchill, and he was, by all accounts, the greatest leader of the twentieth century. The character with which he

> One can acquire everything in solitude—except character.
> STENDHAL

less grace mercy love faith goodness truth freedom hope
orgiveness peace humble holiness obey repent perfect submit
serve fellowship comforter transformed noble character church

The Price of Glory

led the nations was fashioned largely through suffering.

Even Jesus had to be fashioned through suffering, and not just at his death. Hebrews 5:8 says that though Jesus was the sinless son of God, he was fashioned for his destiny by "the things which he suffered" (KJV). Clearly, God wanted to accomplish something in Jesus that could only be done through hardship. But what kind of hardships? Well, Jesus would have suffered the death of his earthly father when he was a young man. He was often misunderstood, so much so that his own family once thought he was "not in his right mind." His best friends betrayed him, and entire crowds tried to kill him. This is not to mention the demonic torment he must have battled all his life. Yet he endured, grew into the man his heavenly Father had called him to be, and so became the source of salvation for all humankind.

> A wife of noble character is her husband's crown, but a disgraceful wife is like decay in his bones.
> **Proverbs 12:4** NIV

🔒

The key to character is found in James 1:2–4: "Whenever trouble comes your way, let it be an opportunity for joy. For when your faith is tested, your endurance has a chance to grow. So let it grow, for when your endurance is fully developed, you will be strong in character and ready for anything" (NLT).

words
to live by

Things you might not know about *character:*

❶ Psychologists and historians studying the factors that lead to success and greatness often conclude that character is a greater indicator of success than intelligence, talent, or beauty.

❶ The classics of Greek literature have influenced the arts and philosophy for generations. Yet scholars have long suggested that Greek philosophy can be summarized in a simple phrase: "Character is destiny."

A talent is formed in stillness, a character in the world's torrent.
JOHANN WOLFGANG VON GOETHE

Sow a thought, and you
   reap an act;
Sow an act, and you reap a
   habit;
Sow a habit, and you reap a
   character;
Sow a character, and you
   reap a destiny.
AUTHOR UNKNOWN

Bad company
corrupts good
character.
I Corinthians 15:33 NIV

God, grant me the grace to endure suffering
with my eyes on you, with trust in my heart,
and with the hope that I will emerge more
clearly fashioned in the image of Jesus.
—Amen.

c h a r · a c · t e r

Laying Hold of Destiny

choice, noun.

1. the outcome of selecting that which is preferred.
2. the result of distinguishing and exercising the best option.
3. that which is approved in preference to others.
4. *Biblical:* the decision that determines the paths of life.
5. *Personal:* the power you are granted to determine your life.

choice

A beautiful picture emerges from the language of Philippians 3:12. Paul wrote that he wanted to take hold of that for which Christ Jesus had taken hold of him. In other words, Paul knew that God had chosen him and, in the words of Acts 26:16, had appeared to him "for this purpose, to make [him] a minister and a witness" (MKJV).

As Paul grew in an understanding of his calling, he yearned to fulfill it. He hungered to accomplish the purpose for which Jesus appeared to him in the first place. This, even as he languished in a Philippian jail, was the passion of his heart.

The picture that the words suggest is touching. Just as a father lifts his little boy in the air so that the child can reach an

Choose this day whom you will serve.
Joshua 24:15 MKJV

words

to live by

apple on a high branch, so God "takes hold" of his children and lifts them to their purpose. Then they can reach for that "upward call," that apple of their destiny.

To put it another way, God chooses you so that you in turn can choose. You have to make a choice, the decision to strain for the goal that God has appointed you for. This is more, though, than just choosing to fulfill your destiny. It is a choosing of God's will all along the road to your destiny.

The fact is, God never wanted robots. He could have made you without a will, without the power of choice. But he already had angels. The Bible seems to indicate that angels can only do the will of God. They are, as one writer has said, "God's holy and awe-inspiring robots." This is overstated, of course, but it makes the point. If all God wanted were beings that did his will unquestioningly, he already had them.

What he wanted were sons and daughters who would choose him, choose his will, and choose to fulfill their purpose. So he took a risk. He created a magnificent world, put a man and a woman in it, and gave them the power to rule over it. In doing so, he also gave them the power to blow it. And they did. They disobeyed God and gave their authority over the earth to the enemy, Satan. That is why, when Satan was tempting Jesus, he showed him all the nations and said, "I will give you all their authority and splendor, for it has been given to me, and I can give it to anyone I want to." Satan had received this

> Life does not give itself to one who tries to keep all its advantages at once. I have often thought morality may perhaps consist solely in the courage of making a choice.
> **Leon Blum**

unless grace mercy love faith goodness truth freedom hope
orgiveness peace humble holiness obey repent perfect submit
erve fellowship comforter transformed noble character church

Choose my instruction instead of silver, knowledge rather than choice gold.
Proverbs 8:10 NIV

authority from the fallen Adam and Eve.

When Jesus defeated Satan on the cross, he took all authority back and began restoring all that had been lost in the fall of Adam and Eve. Among the things he restored was choice. He set humankind free from the domination of Satan, a condition that offered no choice but evil, and gave them the power to choose God again. They were no longer slaves. Now they were sons and daughters, exercising their power to choose righteousness.

This, then, is one of the great mysteries of the Christian life. God has chosen you so that you can choose. And choose you must, for it is how you honor God and take hold of the life that is truly life. You must exercise your liberated will, declare yourself for God's expressed will, and walk out your choices with diligence.

🔒

How do you choose? First, you learn what your choices are from the Bible. Next, you declare yourself, even saying the words aloud and holding them in faith as though they were your own. Finally, you must act and do the deeds your choices demand. Then you will find the flow of power that righteous choice produces. This is the ultimate result of godly choosing.

Things you might not know about *choice:*

❶ Psychologists know that the ability to exercise choice is an essential part of human maturity and a mark of adulthood. The same is true in spiritual maturity.

❶ Martin Luther was the great reformer who sparked the Reformation and restored the truth of the priesthood of all believers to the church. He once said, "Choice is the rudder of our lives as we sail on the seas of God's providence."

The more destined a man believes himself to be, the more boldly he may choose a path for himself.
WINSTON CHURCHILL

The sin is not in having chosen badly but in never having chosen at all.
THEODORE ROOSEVELT

You did not choose me, but I chose you and appointed you to go and bear fruit— fruit that will last.
John 15:16 NIV

God, free me from fear and liberate me to choose and choose boldly your will, your ways, and your glory. Reveal the path chosen for me in your word and let me walk in it as I choose you daily. And I thank you for having chosen me that I may in turn choose you and your will for my life.
—Amen.

choice

church, noun.

1. a body of religious believers.
2. a formal gathering of Christians.
3. a temple or building for Christian worship.
4. **Biblical:** the gathering of those for whom Jesus is Lord.
5. **Personal:** the body of Christians whom you serve and to whom you belong.

church

I will call you Peter, which means "a rock." On this rock I will build my church, and death itself will not have any power over it.
Matthew 16:18 CEV

God has always called out his people. He called Abraham out of Ur of the Chaldees and then called him again from Haran into the Promised Land. He called Moses from the wilderness, Israel from Egypt, and the twelve tribes out of their wandering and into their inheritance. It didn't stop there. He constantly called his people out of their idolatry and, when they wouldn't hear him, he called them back from their punishing captivity time and time again.

Then he decided to issue "the big call." He was tired of the cycles of backsliding, punishment, and return that had defined the history of Israel. He wanted a people who would "bear the fruit" of his kingdom. He wanted a people who would live apart from the ways of the world and for him alone.

words
to live by

So he sent his Son to die for the sins of the world and he sent his Spirit to live in those who were willing to believe. Then he issued the call. To his followers he said, "Go into all the world and make disciples, teaching them what I have commanded you." So they went. They issued the call to the ones who were called, and so God built his church.

This church is the gathering of the called of God. In fact, the Greek word for church, *ekklesia*, means "the called out ones." The called of God are called, first, out of their old lives—days of darkness, of sin, and of the tortures it brings. But the called all know a moment when their hearts melt, understanding dawns, and new life begins on the wings of confession.

The called of God are also called to be together. They have walked alone enough in their lives. Now they are part of a body, of a people who serve God by serving each other with the gifts he has given. The lonely are set in families, the fatherless find the tending they need, and the weary are refreshed by those who love them. It is a family and an army, a structure and a flow, an organism and an organization. And now they belong each of them to one another.

Yet, ultimately, they are called to their Lord, for they are the body of Christ. They are called out to him, and it is his pleasure they seek, his presence they adore, and his glory they reflect. He is their life, and apart from him they are lost and without hope.

The Church has many critics but no rivals.
CHARLES SPURGEON

ness grace mercy love faith goodness truth freedom hope
orgiveness peace humble holiness obey repent perfect submit
serve fellowship comforter transformed noble character church

A People Called Out

I am now rejoicing in my sufferings for your sake, and in my flesh I am completing what is lacking in Christ's afflictions for the sake of his body, that is, the church.
Colossians 1:24 NRSV

This church has been a unique institution in history. It has failed often only to rise again. It has fought itself, divided, and reunited only to split again and again. Yet the church and the gospel it preaches have served as the most unifying force in the history of humankind. Moreover, the church has seldom achieved its earthly ambitions but often fulfilled its heavenly mandate. When the church works, it is glorious. When it does not, it can become a chamber of horrors.

This is the church, and you are called to it. In fact, you are commanded not to "forsake the assembling of yourselves together," but to invest yourself. This is how you grow. You have a destiny, but that destiny is fulfilled in a corporate setting, requires the gifts of others, and will never be achieved apart from the right "fitting" in a body of believers.

To arise to your best, you need the church. The church is where God's presence is known, where God's leaders invest in your growth, and where you'll find the soil of greatness. Give yourself to her, love her, serve her, and take your role in the glorious body of Christ. This is part of who you are in Christ.

words
to live by

Things you might not know about *church:*

❶ Many factors contribute to happiness, and many surveys try to determine what those factors are. The surveys have shown, though, that among those who rate themselves as happy people, church attendance is a primary contributing factor.

❶ Hundreds of programs and millions of dollars have been devoted to turning youth from the temptations that can destroy their lives. Recently, several leading studies have shown that church attendance is a significant influence in keeping youth off drugs, away from criminal activity, and in school.

It were better to be of no church than to be bitter for any.
WILLIAM PENN

The Church faces a generation which is trying to drink its way to prosperity, war its way to peace, spend its way to wealth and enjoy its way to heaven.
ANONYMOUS

Take heed to yourselves, and to all the flock over which the Holy Spirit has made you overseers, to feed the church of God which He has purchased with His own blood.
Acts 20:28 MKJV

God, help me to belong among your people. I have heard the call, both to Jesus and out of the world. Now call me together with others to serve your purposes. Forgive me that I have stood apart from your people with criticism and fear. Make me a functioning member of your body, the church.
—Amen.

church

One Called to Help

com·fort·er, noun.

1. one who gives strength and hope.
2. one who eases grief or trouble.
3. one who administers consolation.
4. *Biblical:* God's Spirit.
5. *Personal:* God's Spirit who dwells in you.

com · fort · er

The Comforter, the Holy Spirit whom the Father will send in My name, He shall teach you all things and bring all things to your remembrance, whatever I have said to you.
John 14:26 MKJV

In the ancient Greek Olympic Games, the marathon was the queen of the events. The 26.2-mile course wound through the countryside villages and back into the large city from which it began. Runners were revered, and the day of the race was attended by huge crowds all along the course. Nothing was as exciting as those last miles of the race, the miles that made champions.

A practice that has long fallen out of fashion today was quite common in the ancient world. A marathoner was allowed to choose someone to run those last miles with him. This friend would not have run the early miles, but would be fresh and waiting at an appointed place to help his companion run the final distance. He would set the pace, encourage his friend, and warn him of pitfalls in the road. He

words
to live by

never stopped speaking to his exhausted charge, but told him of the glory that awaited if he would only give his best.

This companion to the runner was called the *parakletos*, the "one called alongside to help." His job was to make sure that the runner was safe, that the race was finished, and that excellence prevailed. Runners chose their *parakletos* carefully, for they knew these friends made all the difference.

When God chose a word to describe the ministry of his Spirit in your life, he chose this word, *parakletos*. It is often translated "comforter," and this gives the impression of someone who tends your hurts and eases your pains. Certainly, God's Spirit does this.

Yet God's choice of this word to describe the work of the Spirit reveals so much more. God's Spirit is sent to help you run your race. He is comfort, yes, but he is also coach, companion, guide, encourager, teacher, restorer, and forecaster to name just a few of his roles. How wonderful to know that in the exhaustion of life's race, you have the Spirit that Jesus sent you to see that you would finish the race and finish it well.

In fact, this is one of the reasons Jesus said that it was better for him to ascend to the Father: so he could send the Holy Spirit. You can understand the sorrow that Jesus' disciples must have felt. Even today, if you could choose

> The Spirit of God first imparts love; he next inspires hope, and then gives liberty; and that is about the last thing we have in many of our churches.
> Dwight L. Moody

.dness grace mercy love faith goodness truth freedom hope
orgiveness peace humble holiness obey repent perfect submit
serve fellowship comforter transformed noble character church

One Called to Help

I have much more
to say to you,
more than you
can now bear. But
when he, the Spirit
of truth, comes, he
will guide you into
all truth.
John 16:12–13 NIV

to have Jesus bodily at your side, you would probably do so. But Jesus said it was better for him to go. He knew that in his human body, he could not be everywhere; he could not be the *parakletos* for everyone since he could not be everywhere at once. So he went to the Father and sent the Spirit. This was better, he said, for the Spirit would replicate the life of Jesus in you and empower you to finish your course.

As time progressed in the ancient world, this word came to mean something else. When a citizen appeared in court, the legal defender at his side was also called the *parakletos*. He was the advocate, the guardian, and the counsel for the defense. What a beautiful picture this paints of the ministry of God's Spirit. He is with you in your "trials," with you when you are opposed, and with you when you need defending.

🔒

It is no wonder the word "parakletos" is often translated "comforter." What could be of greater comfort than knowing you have God's Spirit at your side, committed to help you defeat your enemies and run your destined race? Then, as Paul said, you will be able to "comfort those in trouble with the comfort we ourselves have received from God."

words
to live by

Things you might not know about *comforter:*

❶ You have heard the phrase "providing aid and comfort to the enemy"? The way the word is used here helps us understand it better. It does not mean making an enemy physically comfortable. It means "aiding him in his purpose." This is how we ought to comfort our fellow believers.

❶ Sometimes the history of words helps us to understand their spiritual application. The English word *comfort* comes from the Latin *comforto*, to relieve. Clearly, God's Spirit has come to "relieve" us of our burdens.

When men surrender themselves to the Spirit of God, they will learn more concerning God and Christ and the Atonement and Immortality in a week, than they would learn in a lifetime, apart from the Spirit.
JOHN BROWN

Come, Holy Ghost, our souls inspire,
And lighten with celestial fire.
RABANUS MAURUS

O my Comforter in sorrow.
Jeremiah 8:18 NIV

God, thank you for Jesus and thank you for your Spirit. I know that the Bible says that if I am led by the Spirit, I am a son of God. Help me to follow the Spirit's leading, to know the Spirit's voice, to heed the Spirit's counsel. I want to be your child and finish the race you have set out for me.
—Amen.

com·fort·er

death, noun.

1. the end of life.
2. the cessation of all vital functions.
3. the state of being inanimate.
4. **Biblical:** the end of the days appointed for a life.
5. **Personal:** the instant your spirit leaves your body.

death

In the cathedrals of Europe, visitors often find an astonishing sight. If they look closely at the columns and the walls, they will see carvings of skulls embedded in the architecture. Given the modern association of skulls with the occult, these carvings are almost offensive. Yet they were not put there to encourage evil. As one church steward explained, "They are there that men might contemplate their mortality."

All throughout church history, it has been a common belief among Christians that they will live better lives if they keep the fact of death in mind. Rather than fear death, they have encouraged each other to think of their lives from the vantage point of the grave, to consider what is truly important and what they will wish their lives had been on the day of their death.

It is better to go to a house of mourning than to go to a house of feasting, for death is the destiny of every man; the living should take this to heart.
Ecclesiastes 7:2 NIV

words
to live by

Indeed, it was common at one point in history for people to sign their letters "Memento Mori"—remember death.

This kind of thinking is only possible for those who have been freed from the fear of death. For those who know that the cross of Jesus has destroyed the power of death and who know that a better life awaits them, death is nothing to fear. But it is something to be remembered. Death will mean the end of the power to do good, the lifting of the pen from the pages of their lives. As Ecclesiastes says, it is good for the living to take death to heart, for then they will live more exceptional lives. This is why Winston Churchill once wrote, "When the notes of life ring false, men should correct them by referring to the tuning fork of death."

Thinking about the day of your death has a power to cut away the unimportant things of life. As you look back on your life from the edge of the grave, you are not likely to wish you had spent more time at the office or watching television. You will not wish you had made more money or experienced more pleasure. More likely, you will wish that you had lived more meaningfully, more deeply. You will almost certainly regret not living on a larger scale, with a greater passion to glorify God and fulfill your destiny. At the moment of your death, if you could have

> Some die without having really lived, while others continue to live, in spite of the fact that they have died.
>
> AUTHOR UNKNOWN

...ness grace mercy love faith goodness truth freedom hope
orgiveness peace humble holiness obey repent perfect submit
serve fellowship comforter transformed noble character church

The Tuning Fork of Life

> Jesus . . . has destroyed death and has brought life and immortality to light through the gospel.
>
> **2 Timothy 1:10** NIV

more time, you would most likely choose to love more fully, make a difference in more lives, give more generously, and devote yourself more completely to your God.

It is this very contemplation of death as an enrichment of life that has made some of the famous speeches of history. In the great Agincourt speech of Shakespeare's *Henry V,* in Lincoln's Gettysburg Address, in Churchill's call to war, and in the stirring statements of leaders from William Wallace to Alfred the Great, the charge to view life from the edge of the grave has moved people to give their best.

Take a moment to ponder your life from the vantage point of death. Imagine how your obituary might read. Imagine a conversation with Jesus on the day of your death. Or perhaps you might divide a sheet into two columns with the details of your calling on one side and how well you are fulfilling it on the other. Certainly, other techniques may come to mind, but the goal is the same: Let the eventuality of death tune your life so that you can live the "life that is truly life."

words
to live by

Things you might not know about *death:*

❶ Death is the second greatest fear among human beings. Fear of speaking in public is the greatest fear. It is interesting that people deeply fear death but seem to do very little to change their lives in light of it.

❶ The most successful armies in the world have often been those whose soldiers have prepared for death, settled their affairs, and decided only to focus on dying well in the service of their cause. The fear of death gone, they were free to fight well.

Only those are fit to live who are not afraid to die.
GENERAL DOUGLAS MACARTHUR

I depart from life as from an inn, and not as from my home.
CICERO

O death, where is your victory? O death, where is your sting?
I Corinthians 15:55 NLT

God, I long to let death be a tuning fork in my life. Help me to view my life from the grave and to live in light of that day. Free me from the fear of death that I might fight the battles of faith with nobility and peace.
—Amen.

death

uness grace mercy love faith goodness truth freedom hope
orgiveness peace humble holiness obey repent perfect submit
serve fellowship comforter transformed noble character church

Fulfilling Your Divine Purpose

---

des·ti·ny, noun.

1. a predetermined course of events.
2. the ultimate fate.
3. a necessary or fixed order of things.
4. **Biblical:** what God has determined to accomplish.
5. **Personal:** the purposes God has set for your life.

des·ti·ny

You heard the gospel and you believed it. You gave your life to Jesus, and you became a Christian. Why?

Perhaps you were drawn to the love that Jesus offers. Or perhaps the preacher told you that God could heal your marriage or get you off drugs or answer the loneliness in your heart. Perhaps you simply wanted to be clean on the inside like the preacher said you could be. And so you became a Christian.

> I press on to take hold of that for which Christ Jesus took hold of me.
> **Philippians 3:12** NIV

You joined a church and learned the Bible and fell in love with Jesus. And it was wonderful! Nothing was the same after that. Yet, as time went by, you sensed there was something more. Not more than Jesus, just more that he could do with your life. You couldn't shake it, that inner hunger to be more in his hands.

words
to live by

All this is normal, for these are the stirrings of destiny. It is what happens when you have been a believer for a while and come to know that you were made for a purpose. You were not saved just to be saved; you were also saved to achieve something God has determined for your life. It is what happens when you come to know that you have a destiny.

Paul had a destiny and God wasted no time telling him about it. As soon as God knocked Paul from his horse on the Damascus Road and warned him not to persecute the newborn Church, he said, "I have appeared to you for this purpose." God began to tell Paul what his life would be about. Later, Paul understood that God had "set me apart from birth," and it made him want to take hold of the reason God had saved him in the first place: to go to the Gentiles and turn them from darkness to light.

This sense of divine purpose was the fuel behind Paul's ministry. Words like *appointed, called, sent,* and *ordained* fell freely from his lips and his pen. Even when he suffered persecution, he told the churches not to worry about him because he was "destined" for such hardship. Clearly, Paul wanted to glorify Jesus by fulfilling his destiny, the purpose set for his life.

It would be easy to think that only people like Paul and those who stand in pulpits have

There's no such thing as chance; and what to us seems merest accident springs from the deepest source of destiny.
JOHANN FRIEDRICH VON SCHILLER

Your eyes have seen my unformed substance; and in Your book they were all written the days that were ordained for me, when as yet there was not one of them.
Psalm 139:16 NASB

destinies. But that isn't true. All believers have been fashioned with a purpose, which was set before they were even born. All believers have been shaped in the womb according to that divine purpose. And all believers have been called to take hold of that for which Jesus has taken hold of them—to fulfill their destiny, their divine purpose.

Imagine what life would be like if you had the same attitude Paul had. God performed miracles at Paul's hands and Paul preached the gospel throughout the known world, and yet Paul's ultimate passion was to glorify Jesus by fulfilling his purpose. Paul's kind of attitude can keep you from settling for less than you were made for. And it can move you to live the exceptional life you were designed to live.

①

You may take the first step toward your higher destiny when you become dissatisfied with the norm of your life. This dissatisfaction is a deep hunger that God creates to move you toward his purposes. Your job is to turn that hunger to prayer rather than to frustration, and to be ready for God to show you a new avenue for your life, an avenue filled with the greater work he created you to accomplish.

words
to live by

Things you might not know about *destiny:*

❶ Human beings seem to have an innate need for a sense of destiny. Psychologists have explained that suicide and depression result from a loss of purpose, but that one of the primary ingredients of mental health is a vital sense of an assured future.

❶ Among the most common themes cited by great Christian leaders like George Whitefield or Martin Luther as the fuel for their achievements is an unshakable sense of having been made for a unique purpose.

I felt as if I were walking with destiny, and that all my past life had been but a preparation for this hour and this trial.
WINSTON CHURCHILL

Heroes who shape a generation are most commonly those who believe themselves destined for greatness.
CHRISTOPHER SYNN

We are His workmanship, created in Christ Jesus for good works, which God prepared beforehand that we should walk in them.
Ephesians 2:10 NASB

God, let me take hold of that for which Christ Jesus has taken hold of me. Fulfill in me every purpose you have ordained for me so that I may be pleasing to you.
—Amen.

d e s · t i · n y

dis·ci·ple, noun.

1. a follower.
2. one who accepts discipline toward a goal.
3. one devoted to a teacher or a body of truth.
4. **Biblical:** an obedient follower of Jesus.
5. **Personal:** what you are when you welcome God's discipline.

dis·ci·ple

Are students better than their teacher? But when they are fully trained, they will be like their teacher.
Luke 6:40 CEV

You became a Christian because you believed. You had an inner knowing that what you were hearing was true. You found yourself believing in a God who sent his son to die for the sins of the world. You had heard this before but it never meant much to you. Something changed, though. It came to mean everything. You also found yourself believing that he died for you and that if you would acknowledge what you believe and devote yourself to him, Jesus would live in you, change you, and give you the life that is truly life. This you had to have, so you became a believer.

You kept believing. You got around people who loved the Scriptures, and you soon heard more things to believe. You grew in your beliefs, not just in believing them more passionately but in having a more full-bodied understanding of what you believed. This is how you grew in your faith.

The Disciplines of Destiny

words
to live by

Then a new understanding crept into your mind. You soon realized that among the things you should believe is, you were made with a purpose. You have a destiny, a unique role God wants you to play. It was exciting to learn this, and you wondered how you could indeed "take hold of that for which Christ Jesus had taken hold" of you.

Soon you learned how destiny is fulfilled. You had to enroll in school. Not a college or university-type school, but the school of God. You quickly began to understand that those who are going to fulfill the purposes of God for their lives have to yield to his training program. It means recognizing that God will use everything in your life to shape you. It means understanding that nothing is too small for God to use, that in fact it is your faithfulness in the small that determines how you will be trusted with the weighty.

To put it simply, you had been a believer. Now you had to become a disciple also. You had to welcome the disciplines of God sent to chisel you into the image of Jesus, into that useful tool of destiny. You learned that he only disciplines those he loves, that he allows hardship to do its work in you only to fashion you. Suddenly you found him using relationships, schedules, duties, those in authority over you, and even your pleasures to train you. And sometimes it wasn't pleasant. As one Texan said, "He fixes a fix to fix us." He creates situations you would normally run from to wean you

> We may be doing Jesus an injustice in stressing the fact that He so frequently said "Go . . . !" His first word to His disciples was not "Go" but "Come."
> **AUTHOR UNKNOWN**

uness grace mercy love faith goodness truth freedom hope
orgiveness peace humble holiness obey repent perfect submit
serve fellowship comforter transformed noble character church

If any man come to me, and hate not his father, and mother, and wife, and children, and brethren, and sisters, yea, and his own life also, he cannot be my disciple.

Luke 14:26 KJV

from the comfortable and send you into the unfamiliar realms of faith. This is what brings growth and what makes you more the disciple of his dreams.

Now you have grown from being a believer only to being a disciple also. Now what you believe you find worked into your life by the processes of God. You are being shaped in his image, and it is glorious. Not easy. Not always comfortable. But glorious to be increasingly freed from what you were to become what he has made you to be.

🔒

The path to discipleship is powered by the question, "What is next?" What is that next lesson, that next crisis God is planning to perfect you in him? You can never settle, never be satisfied with your growth. You have to move from faith to faith. Every day you take up the cross you love and look to see where Jesus is taking you. For you are a disciple, one of those who have welcomed the disciplines of their God. And you intend to win your world by welcoming the chiseling work of his hands.

Things you might not know about *disciple:*

❶ Sociologists have suggested the theory that everyone is being discipled by someone or something. The question is, "Who is discipling you, and where is it taking you?"

❶ In a recent book that ranked the most influential people in history, Mohammad ranked above Jesus. The reason, according to the authors? Jesus' disciples have failed to do what he said. Muhammad's succeeded.

To make a disciple is to make the great life for life exchange, to imprint the good in us upon those who will make that good even better.
JAMES HOßWARD

The disciple endures discipline in the pursuit of destiny.
CHRISTOPHER SYNN

If you hold to my teaching, you are really my disciples. Then you will know the truth, and the truth will set you free.
John 8:31–32 NIV

God, I want to believe all your truth and have that truth worked into my life. I want to be your disciple. Use the circumstances of my life. Shape me. Make me pleasing in your sight and useful in your hands.
—Amen.

d i s · c i · p l e

dis·pute, noun.

1. an argument.
2. a question.
3. the act of disproving through reasoning.
4. **Biblical:** a disagreement or contest of ideas.
5. **Personal:** an inevitability when living with human beings.

dis·pute

> On my own body
> are scars that prove
> I belong to Christ
> Jesus. So I don't
> want anyone to
> bother me anymore.
> **Galatians 6:17** CEV

It is hard to read. Paul and Barnabas, the great missionary team commissioned by God's Spirit in Acts 13, those great defenders of truth at the Council of Jerusalem in Acts 15, were arguing with each other. The issue was Mark, the young man who abandoned them on their first missionary journey. Now it was time for a second missionary journey, and Barnabas wanted to take Mark along. Paul wouldn't have it. The boy left them hanging once, and Paul wouldn't give him a chance to do it again. Barnabas, the more tenderhearted, thought Mark should be given another try. The Bible doesn't hide the tension. Acts 15:39 says that between Paul and Barnabas "there arose such a sharp disagreement that they separated from one another" (NASB). You know the rest of the story. Those two great men of God never worked together again.

Disputes happen, even for great men and women of God. They are part of life.

Because humans are flawed, attempts to get along together are bumpy, filled with good but also beset with tension and hurt. The Bible makes it clear: "Offenses will come." As long as you are in this life and in contact with other human beings—particularly if you are trying to work closely with them—disputes will happen. The challenge isn't avoiding them. The challenge is to go through them redemptively, to have conflicts that get resolved with friendships and Christian unity intact.

The problem is, humans tend to see all conflict as evil and so avoid it at all costs. This usually means that they simply let tensions build until they become explosive. Unity is damaged, friendships are destroyed, and the faith gets a black eye.

The truth is, low level "explosions" or conflicts that are handled well can actually build unity and promote maturity among believers. Think about it. You drive a car that is fueled by small explosions, and you're glad for them. You fly in planes that are kept in the air by small explosions. That's how engines and jets work. They create small, manageable explosions that fuel the vehicle. This is exactly what disputes among believers can do if they are handled well.

It were endless to dispute upon everything that is disputable.
WILLIAM PENN

Wisdom for dealing with disputes springs from the pages of the New Testament. Believers should avoid unnecessary disputes, Paul wrote. Then, if a disagreement arises, Christians should handle

A Necessary Correction

Starting a quarrel is like breaching a dam; so drop the matter before a dispute breaks out.
Proverbs 17:14 NIV

the matter in a spirit of love, humility, and gentleness. If they can't work out a problem one on one, they should involve a third party and then, if there is no resolution, ask the church for help. Most disputes don't have to go this far, though. They are problems of character. People demand their rights, insist on vindication, or can't let an offense go. The solution is to rise above the lesser self and become the valiant Christian you are made to be.

Disputes are going to happen. They don't have to mean disaster. In fact, they can make a friendship stronger, a family tighter, and a church more unified if they are handled in the clean, redemptive way Jesus would. Don't run from disputes. Run through them with grace and watch the good that comes from it.

words
to live by

Things you might not know about *dispute:*

● Business managers constantly study the factors that produce effective leadership. Among the skills they rate most highly is the ability to avoid and resolve conflict.

● After studying the factors that lead to missionary failure, a major Christian missionary organization recently reported that more than seventy percent of all missionary endeavors are jeopardized by unresolved disputes among those in the field.

He could distinguish and divide
A hair 'twixt south and southwest side,
On either which he would dispute,
Confute, change hands, and still confute.
SAMUEL BUTLER

Our disputants put me in mind of the skuttle fish, that when he is unable to extricate himself, blackens all the water about him, till he becomes invisible.
JOSEPH ADDISON

Accept him whose faith is weak, without passing judgment on disputable matters.
Romans 14:1 NIV

God, I know that I can be petty and small. Please help me to rise above and to allow low-level conflicts righteously resolved to propel me to my destiny. I long to forgive, long to heal, and long to walk in unity. May I bring glory to Jesus in the disputes of my life.
—Amen.

d i s · p u t e

ed·i·fy, verb.

1. to instruct or improve spiritually.
2. to improve in moral and religious matters.
3. to teach and inspire.
4. *Biblical:* to build the inner being by word and prayer.
5. *Personal:* to uplift other believers.

e d · i · fy

To Build the Inner House

Edify one another.

1 Thessalonians 5:11

MKJV

words
to live by

You are under construction. You are constantly being made into what God designed you for, but you will never be complete in this life.

This process of emerging into maturity requires more than what you can provide yourself. Oh, you can study Scripture, pray, go to church, and do the right things. But you need more. You need what other people with complementary gifts can impart. What you need them to do is to edify you, just as they need the same from you.

This word *edify* is an older word the modern world doesn't use much anymore. It is used in the King James Version of the Bible, but most modern translations don't include it. Instead, they use words like *encourage* or *inspire*. These are good, but they don't mean the same thing.

The word *edify* means specifically "to build the house," and this is a very apt description of what Christian growth is like. You can be thankful the Holy Spirit chose to use this word. When something is built, materials are added that aren't there originally. People with skills you don't have must ply their trades, and each piece must go in at the right time. There must also be a plan, a blueprint, and each part of the plan must be followed in order for the ultimate structure to be complete.

This image is a perfect illustration of how you grow spiritually. God has a plan for your life, a destiny ordained long ago. Some gifts you had when you entered this world and some you acquired through experience. Some resources God put in you and others have to be put in by people. This is how you are edified, built up into the "house" for God's Spirit that you are made to be.

The problem that often arises when people use the word *edify* is that they tend to understand edification merely as short-term inspiration. They think of it as encouragement or excitement that lasts only for a short while. But edification is meant to produce fruit that lasts. Like the building of a house, it is a lengthy process that produces something long lasting. When you edify someone, you put into their hearts understanding, insight, courage, loving reflections of themselves, and strength that should last for years.

The Marine Corps used to say that it could "build men." This is exactly what the church is called to do. Christians build by speaking truth, using the gifts God has

> Our words are meant to inspire others to greatness. It is sin to use the spirit of another man as the garbage pail for our bitter spew. Men ought to be better for having been in our presence.
> MARCUS JAMES

ness grace mercy love faith goodness truth freedom hope
orgiveness peace humble holiness obey repent perfect submit
erve fellowship comforter transformed noble character church

given them to make permanent additions to the lives of others. Yes, you inspire and encourage, but you do something more. You edify, you build the house of the heart so God can inhabit.

Christians can edify each other because they do not see each other only in terms of who they are now. They love each other as they are, but every believer envisions his fellow believer as mature in the image of Jesus. So they have a vision for each other, a mental picture of what they can become. A Christian doesn't think of, say, Sally as forever the Sally she is now. They think of her as a Sally version of Jesus. The Christian's role is to contribute what they can to the process.

All things are lawful for me, but all things are not expedient: all things are lawful for me, but all things edify not.
1 Corinthians 10:23
KJV

Think for a moment about how you can edify those around you. What building material, what spiritual gift, do you have that can help to mold them into the image of Jesus? How might you inspire, instruct, and impart a sense of courage to your fellow believers? This is what it means to edify another human being, and you can be sure that God has given you some unique gift for contributing to the lives of others.

words
to live by

Things you might not know about *edify:*

1 Battlefield chaplains have reported that the final words of dying soldiers are often either the hurtful or the affirming words spoken by parents years before. Clearly, the words spoken by parents and friends live long and shape life to the end.

1 Psychologists have long argued that a human being only comes to know who he is in the picture of himself painted by the words of others. This is as true for a distorted picture, painted through cursing and hatred, as much as it is for words of affirmation and blessing.

The old word "edify" means to build, and we build a man by believing in his purpose, investing in his future, and chiseling what we have of God in his soul.
HAROLD PAUL

Edify, inspire, and inflame the soul with holy passion: this is the duty we owe our fellow Christians.
BOB MUMFORD

Let us therefore follow after the things which make for peace, and things wherewith one may edify another.
Romans 14:19 KJV

God, just as your words have formed my concept of who I am as a believer, so let my words frame the destinies of those around me. Keep me from the coarse jest, the hurtful joke, and the poisonous barb. Let my words be a fountain of life for many.
—Amen.

e d · i · f y

en·cour·age, verb.

1. to inspire with courage, spirit, or hope.
2. to spur on.
3. to increase confidence of success.
4. **Biblical:** to instill boldness for right action.
5. **Personal:** to infuse or be infused with righteous passion.

en · cour · age

Have you ever had this experience? You spend what should have been a pleasant hour of conversation with a friend. Yet when you are done, instead of feeling satisfied and happy you feel horrible. Faith has drained out of you, the world seems cold and tragic, and you have a hard time having any sense of hope or expectation for the future.

Finally, brothers . . .
encourage yourselves.
2 Corinthians 13:11
MKJV

This happens all too often. You open yourself to hear the words of others, and then those words become a spew of the negative, the impure, and the cowardly. You just generally feel like you have taken an elevator several floors down into your lowest possible self. The truth is, your soul has been used as someone else's garbage pail, the receptacle of their destructive refuse.

Yet you have probably had this experience also. You spend time with a friend, and when you part you feel like you could change the world all by yourself. You've

The Power to Impart Purpose

words
to live by

heard stories of God's work in the lives of others, heard Scripture quoted and been helped to think about the good in life and the joy of living large for God. You've experienced what it means for someone to care about you deeply. You're changed, and all you did was spend time with a friend.

What you've experienced in this last example is the power of *encouragement*. People use this word in so many ways that they often lose the meaning. They encourage someone to mow the yard, encourage them not to be rude, and encourage them when they've had a bad day. All these uses are legitimate, since one sense of the word is "to persuade."

The other, more biblical sense of the word *encourage* is the one people desperately need in their lives. It means "to impart boldness for good, to inspire, to light the fires of the soul." It is more than persuasion and more than a light form of comfort. It is what happens when someone makes a positive, motivating deposit in the heart of another.

Encouragement is critically important to a successful Christian life. You live in a world with negative messages. The media are full of a "what's the use, let's just pleasure life away" kind of ethic. Beyond this, most people hear more negative about themselves than they ought to. People react to you in anger, authority figures speak harsh words that embed themselves deeply in you, and even loved ones sometimes inadvertently send

> Let [a woman] receive encouragement for the proper cultivation of all her powers.
> **LUCRETIA MOTT**

The Power to Impart Purpose

arrows into your heart, arrows that carry distorted messages of who you are.

Encouragement is the antidote. True encouragement is rooted in the understanding that words are carriers. They carry the power to paint pictures of possibilities and to deposit all the forces that fuel a virtuous life. Words are like little train cars, filled with cargo. When they enter your heart, they dump their load. This is why the Bible constantly encourages you to be careful of who you spend time with and to be cautious about what you hear. Words don't go into one ear and out the other. They go into the inner being and become part of how you see yourself. You have to be choosy about your listening diet.

Encourage one another daily, as long as it is called Today, so that none of you may be hardened by sin's deceitfulness.
Hebrews 3:13 NIV

Think for a moment about your conversations and how they make you feel. Is someone using your spirit as a garbage pail? Do you leave the presence of a friend feeling tempted and burdened? This friend is doing the opposite of encouragement. Now think of those whose presence you leave feeling ennobled and strong. These people practice encouragement, and you not only need more of such friends in your life, but you need to be just this kind of friend for those God has entrusted to you.

words
to live by

Things you might not know about *encouragement:*

❶ Among the list of reasons that marriages often decay, counselors have listed the inability of spouses to encourage each other. Strong marriages, they say, are made of people who have the ability to stoke the inner fires of their mates.

❶ A survey of the traits of the most popular students in high schools reveals that their most valued characteristic was their ability to encourage others. Fellow students felt they were better for being in the presence of their friend, and this is what made others want to be around them.

Let us then animate and encourage each other.
GEORGE WASHINGTON

To encourage your brother means just that: put courage in the brother and the brother in courage.
RICE BROOCKS

Saul's son Jonathan went to David at Horesh and helped him find strength in God.
I Samuel 23:16 NIV

God, let me not disillusion more than I encourage.
Let me impart power and boldness where I can. Let
me fulfill your ministry of encouragement that those
I touch may fulfill their destinies.
—Amen.

en · cour · age

ness grace mercy love faith goodness truth freedom hope
orgiveness peace humble holiness obey repent perfect submit
serve fellowship comforter transformed noble character church

e·ter·ni·ty, *noun.*

1. the realm outside of time.
2. the existence that is without beginning or end.
3. the state after death
4. **Biblical:** the infinite expanse in which God dwells.
5. **Personal:** the timeless, spaceless realm for which you were made.

e · ter · ni · ty

The Realm Your Soul Yearns For

He has made everything beautiful in His time; also He has set eternity in their heart.
Ecclesiastes 3:11 MKJV

Do you feel like a misfit in this life? Do you feel like you were made for another existence altogether but were dropped into this one by mistake? You aren't alone. Most people feel this way. They feel pressed into this life while something inside reaches for a broader existence elsewhere. They rail against death, rage against time, and resist with all their hearts the tragedies and disappointments of this life.

This is actually good news. It confirms that you weren't made for this life alone. You were made for eternity.

Imagine for a moment what many people still believe: that this life is all there is. Life has no meaning outside of what a person can see. People are born, they live, and then they die. That's it: no higher meaning, no bigger picture. Life has its beauty and life has its horrors and they both pass at death when life ends. The writer of Ecclesiastes could envision this

words
to live by

kind of thinking and came to one conclusion: If this is true, life is meaningless.

Yet while you once believed this might be true, something inside of you pushed against it. The fit wasn't right. You couldn't easily settle into believing that this world is all there is. Your heart reached for something beyond.

Now you know why. A realm beyond this life does exist, one beyond space and time and all you see about you. It is called eternity, and it is the realm where God dwells. In that realm of infinite existence, that realm in which time is not measured, God fashioned you. But before he put you in this world he ruined you. He put a bit of eternity in your heart. He didn't want this world to be your final home. He didn't want you to settle. So he put the nature of eternity in you and then placed you in a world far more restricted than eternity. He knew you would always yearn for more.

The good news is, though, that to feel misfit in this world is to be normal. You are a misfit. You were fitted for life in another realm, and you will return to that realm eventually. In the meantime, you aren't cut off from eternity. You have eternal life by knowing God now. Jesus said in his prayer in John 17:3 that "this is eternal life: that they may know you, the only true God, and Jesus Christ, whom you have sent" (NIV).

> Learn to hold loosely all that is not eternal.
> A. MAUDE ROYDEN

The Realm Your Soul Yearns For

Jesus came to restore you to the life you were made for. You are an eternal creature, so he awakened the eternity in your heart, seated you in heavenly places by faith, and called you to an eternal relationship with him. He put his eternal Spirit in you, gave you his eternal word, and called you to pray the powers of eternity into the narrow confines of this limited world.

So you are like an expatriate, living in the authority and power of your home though you are yet abroad. The Bible says you are a stranger and a pilgrim in this life. As C. S. Lewis said, "These are the shadow lands. Real life has yet to begin."

Remember, O LORD, Your tender mercies and your loving-kindnesses; for they are from eternity.

Psalm 25:6 MKJV

What good news this all is. You can be free of trying to fit. You never will. Instead you can focus your energies on doing his will on earth as it's being done in eternity, your home. This frees you to enjoy the oddities, suffer the pains, and never have to wonder if this life is all that exits. It isn't, but while it goes on, the eternity that is your real home gives it all meaning.

words
to live by

Things you might not know about *eternity*:

❶ Though we live for eternity, some of the God-given responsibilities we have on earth won't exist in heaven. Marriage is one of them. Matthew 22:30 tells us that humans won't marry in heaven.

❶ Sometimes foreign words help us to better understand the meaning of our own language, especially in matters of religion. For example, the wonderfully expressive word one African tribe uses for *eternity* translates "the village without time."

Eternity is not something that begins after you are dead. It is going on all the time. We are in it now.
CHARLOTTE PERKINS GILMAN

He who has no vision of eternity has no hold on time.
THOMAS CARLYLE

All His works are known to God from eternity.
Acts 15:18 MKJV

God, how I have squirmed with the ill-fit of this life. Forgive me. I wasn't made for this life alone. Help me to resolve this in my heart and live fully in this life until I can be with you in eternity.
—Amen.

e · t e r · n i · t y

fear, noun.

1. a loss of courage.
2. the painful anticipation of some impending evil.
3. the agitation that accompanies a sense of doom.
4. *Biblical:* an intense desire to flee.
5. *Personal:* what you feel when you expect harm
   to befall you.

f e a r

God has not given us
the spirit of fear, but
of power and of love
and of a sound mind.
2 Timothy 1:7 MKJV

The great generals of history, and the history of warfare itself, have together taught a vital key to victory in battle. In fact, this key is taught in all the historic military colleges: at West Point, at Sandhurst in England, and at Saint Cyr in France. In each of these schools, that classic work of strategy by Sun Tzu, called *The Art of War*, is studied closely. This revered book teaches a truth that every student is expected to know and practice. It is this: The best way to win a battle is by never having to fight it, by convincing your enemy he can never win.

The devil knows this strategy and uses it against you. He knows that you have a power in you that is able to do more that you can ask or imagine. He knows you have the mind of Christ, that you have weapons that are mighty through God for the pulling down of strongholds, and that you have power to destroy darkness. In other words, he knows that if you fight,

words
to live by

Freeing the Cowardly Lion Within

you will win. So he uses the oldest tactic in the military manuals. He uses fear to keep you from fighting. He makes you so afraid of the pain that you are unwilling to reach for the glory. To put it simply, he gives you a "spirit of fear" and lets it go to work.

This spirit of fear plays on every painful thing that has ever happened to you. It reminds you of how much life hurts, of what terrible and unjust things are happening all around you. It paints graphic pictures of what might happen and haunts you with images that drain you of all faith and courage. People often speak of being "paralyzed by fear," and it is an apt phrase. Fear does paralyze, for that is what it is sent to do. It makes you freeze in your worry, become immobile in your contemplation of the pain to come. It is meant to keep you from the battle.

What you have to know is, fear comes from a kind of meditation. In fact, fear is connected to worry. Fear grows in a soul that is forever contemplating evil possibilities, that is forever worrying about what horrible thing might happen. The problem is, people become what they behold. In other words, what they think about plants seeds in their souls that grow until they take over the gardens of their hearts. When this happens, fear dominates them and they fall.

Look at the example of Peter. He saw Jesus walk on water and he asked him if he could do it also. Jesus said simply, "Come."

Some people are so afraid to die that they never begin to live.
HENRY VAN DYKE

79

aness grace mercy love faith goodness truth freedom hope
orgiveness peace humble holiness obey repent perfect submit
erve fellowship comforter transformed noble character church

Freeing the Cowardly Lion Within

There is no fear in love, but perfect love casts out fear, because fear has torment. He who fears has not been perfected in love.
1 John 4:18 MKJV

Peter got out of the boat and began to walk on the water. It was the greatest moment of his life. And then he saw something. He saw "that the waves were boisterous" and the "wind was strong." He began to sink. Jesus rescued him but said, "You of little faith, what were you looking at when you doubted?" That's how the original language reads, and it clears up the meaning greatly. You see, you can't walk on water even when it is calm! Peter was walking on water because Jesus said "Come." But Peter began looking at the wind and waves, assumed they could make him sink, and got his mind off of the fact that Jesus had said "Come." Fear entered his heart, and he sank.

🔒

What you must do is battle that spirit of fear by believing the Scriptures more than what you see. You also have to take every thought captive so that worry doesn't plant its evil in your soul. Then you can take hold of the love, power, and sound mind that God intends to replace a spirit of fear.

words
to live by

etcetera . . .

Things you might not know about *fear*:

❶ New Year's resolutions reveal a great deal about the kind of changes people want to make in their lives. Consistently, the change most Americans want to make—just behind losing weight—is getting free from some form of fear.

❶ Increasingly, modern culture deals with the problems of the inner life with medication. The American Medical Association reports that more prescriptions for behavior-modifying drugs are written to combat fear and worry than to deal with any other symptoms.

Fear is pain arising from the anticipation of evil.
ARISTOTLE

Do something every day that scares you.
ELEANOR ROOSEVELT

The fear of man brings a snare, but whoever puts his trust in the LORD shall be safe.
Proverbs 29:25 MKJV

fear

God, I want to live free of fear. Please, remove this spirit of fear from my life. Help me to change my meditations so that I think about your truth rather than what I dread. Help me to have faith for the battles I am called to fight so that I can be pleasing in your sight.
—Amen.

fel·low·ship, noun.

1. a community of interest, activity, feeling, or experience.
2. the state of being a fellow or associate.
3. a company of equals or friends.
4. **Biblical:** the life or experience in common.
5. **Personal:** the life you have in common with others.

fel·low·ship

If you have been in church world for any length of time at all, you are probably familiar with the term *fellowship*. People use it to describe time together. It means a potluck meal in the fellowship hall or coffee with a friend. If you have someone to dinner and have no particular plan, you may say, "Come over. We're just going to fellowship." It means hang out, sit around, or just be together.

In light of the biblical meaning of the word *fellowship*, the way the modern world uses the word isn't wrong, it just isn't enough. The Greek word for fellowship is *koinonia*. It means "having in common, or communion." It doesn't mean just hanging out together or spending some enjoyable time with others. It means having a life in common, what you have jointly with others. Clearly, it refers not to a mere social connection but to an overlapping of life or intimacy of shared experience that produces what can only be

They were continuing steadfastly in the apostles' doctrine, and in fellowship and in the breaking of the loaves, and in prayers.
Acts 2:42 MKJV

described as a "communion."

The definition found in one lexicon may help even more. It tells says that *koinonia* is "that which is the outcome of fellowship." In other words, fellowship is more than just hanging out together. It is what happens when people hang out with a view toward growing together. It is the result of godly fellowship, the fruit of investment in each other: the condition that results from having a common life with others.

This definition certainly helps to put the common use of the word in proper perspective. People say *fellowship* to describe half of the process: the social part. The word actually means what that social part, lived in the Spirit of God, produces. This is what people so desperately need in their churches.

Have you ever had this experience? You are in a crowd and people are being nice and sociable, but you feel very lonely. Every encounter with another human being seems surface and leaves you unfulfilled. You almost feel like you have to leave the crowd to find something "human."

This is what fellowship is apart from the communion it is meant to produce. It is asking someone how things are going but then not helping to bear his or her burden when things aren't going so well. It is the occasional phone call rather than the shared life, the open wallet rather than the open home. It is living in distant "accountability"

Wherein lies happiness?
In that which becks
Our ready minds to
fellowship divine,
A fellowship with
essence; till we shine,
Full alchemiz'd, and
free of space. Behold
The clear religion
of heaven!

JOHN KEATS

...ness grace mercy love faith goodness truth freedom hope
forgiveness peace humble holiness obey repent perfect submit
serve fellowship comforter transformed noble character church

The Common Life

If we walk in the
light, as He is in
the light, we have
fellowship with
one another, and
the blood of Jesus
Christ His Son
purifies us from
all sin.

1 John 1:7 MKJV

rather than so close to another human being that you know their life without them having to say a word.

Fellowship is what everyone hopes for. It is what people admire in movies when a "band of brothers" serves some glorious purpose together. It is what they love when someone takes a bullet for a friend. And it is what they are so moved by in the lives of World War II veterans, that "greatest generation," who faced death in foxholes together. They love each other in a way that only those who have served together in arms can understand.

God has called you to a fellowship that is as intense and tender as anything you've seen in the movies or admired among veterans. He hasn't called you to live alone, but to have life in common with people who make you better for their presence. Being alone from time to time is normal. Being lonely all the time isn't normal. Find the Christian fellowship that helps to make you what you are made to be.

words
to live by

Things you might not know about *fellowship:*

❶ There is an interesting truth that comes from the field of developmental psychology. People come to understand who they are only in the reflection of how others see them. This means that true maturity is only possible as a product of true fellowship.

❶ People go to church to find God and to find spiritual family. Surveys reveal that people leave churches if they find no true fellowship whether they sense God's presence there or not. A recent survey revealed that the single greatest complaint about the churches Americans attend is "a lack of true fellowship."

He who has no stomach to this fight
Let him depart
His passport shall be made and crowns
for convoy put into his purse
We would not die in that man's company
Who fears his fellowship to die with us.
WILLIAM SHAKESPEARE

Fellowship is the union of the trinity attempted among flawed but forgiving mankind.
CHRISTOPHER SYNN

I thank my God . . .
that the fellowship
of your faith may
operate in a full
knowledge of
every good thing in
you in Christ Jesus.
Philemon 1:4, 6 MKJV

God, I have been hurt by people and am tempted to live in isolation. Heal my heart and deliver me from my loner ways. Help me to become part of your body and invest myself in the fellowship that is more than social, but deeply healing and spiritual.
—Amen.

fel·low·ship

ness grace mercy love faith goodness truth freedom hope
orgiveness peace humble holiness obey repent perfect submit
serve fellowship comforter transformed noble character church

for·give·ness, noun.

1. the act of pardoning, of overlooking an offense.
2. the act of sending away a wrong or rejecting it.
3. the state of being free from penalty.
4. **Biblical:** the act of remitting sin.
5. **Personal:** the compassion that erases the heart's memory of wrongs suffered.

for·give·ness

Most people have had a fantasy that plays something like this:

You are seated on something that feels like a throne, in a large, ornate room. You are wrapped in an aura of nobility, a kind and slightly concerned look upon your face. People who have wronged you through the years are before you in a long line. They have all come before you on this day because they have all suddenly realized how horribly they have treated you. They are repentant and tearful. They kneel before you, begging your forgiveness. You extend your hand. . . .

Sound familiar? How many times has a scene like this played in your mind and given you just the right feeling of reconciliation tinged with vengeance? How wonderful it felt!

But there is a problem.

You see, if you secretly long for a scene like this, it means that you secretly wait for a debt to be paid. And if you

> If you forgive men when they sin against you, your heavenly Father will also forgive you. But if you do not forgive men their sins, your Father will not forgive your sins.
> Matthew 6:14–15 NIV

secretly wait for a debt to be paid, it means you haven't forgiven.

"But I have forgiven them," you protest. "I have said the words and refused to speak of it again. I have even hugged them, for heaven's sake! What more do you want?!"

What you have dispensed, though, is "technical forgiveness." You forgave from the will and the mind, but the heart held the offense and still demands its due. You can almost picture a little referee popping up in the corner of your mind. He makes the T sign with his hands and shouts, "Technical forgiveness." You said the words but didn't let it go.

In the New Testament two main words for forgiveness are used. One means "to send away" *(aphiemi)*. The High Priest would lay his hands upon a scapegoat, convey to the goat the sins of the people, and then "send it away" into the wilderness (Leviticus 16:10). Of course, this is exactly what God the Father did in placing upon God the Son the sins of the world. But it is also what you are to do when you forgive. Send the offense away. Forever.

The second word means "to release someone" or "to set someone free" *(apoluo)*. The word refers to setting someone free from prison, which paints a picture of its meaning. When you hold someone in unforgiveness, it is as if you have put that person in prison. Until you forgive that person, he or she cannot be set free.

May I tell you why it seems to me a good thing for us to remember wrong that has been done us? That we may forgive it.
CHARLES DICKENS

...dness grace mercy love faith goodness truth freedom hope
orgiveness peace humble holiness obey repent perfect submit
serve fellowship comforter transformed noble character church

The Power to Set Free

The amazing thing is, when you hold anyone in prison, you are in prison as well. It is almost as if you are standing just outside the prison cells of people you haven't forgiven. You look at them and enjoy the fact that they are bound because they offended you so cruelly. Then you look up and see that you, too, are in a larger cell that holds you as well as them.

You have to send the offense away. If you have been drawing pleasure from bringing them to mind and envisioning your justification, torturing them, as it were, with the unforgiving fantasies of your mind, you must stop. You are only deepening the wound.

Be kind and compassionate to one another, forgiving each other, just as in Christ God forgave you.
Ephesians 4:32 NIV

Want to be free? Send the offense away and treat your offender as if it never happened. Then your offense is sent away and you are treated as if it never happened. Then you are free and those who have wronged you are free, too.

words
to live by

Things you might not know about *forgiveness*:

1 Psychologists have concluded that the *forgiveness* that is so necessary to mental health is impossible for most people until they find some sense of compassion for the frailties of those who have wronged them.

1 Psychosomatic illnesses, or physical illnesses that originate in the emotions, have received a great deal of attention in medical literature of late. Numerous studies identify the connection between diseases like cancer and arthritis and strong feelings of anger, regret, and bitterness.

Little, vicious minds abound with anger and revenge, and are incapable of feeling the pleasure of forgiving their enemies.
LORD CHESTERFIELD

He that cannot forgive others, breaks the bridge over which he himself must pass if he would ever reach heaven; for every one has need to be forgiven.
GEORGE HERBERT

Love your enemies and pray for those who persecute you, that you may be sons of your Father in heaven.
Matthew 5:44–45 NIV

God, forgive me for the unforgiveness in my life.
Help me to find compassion for the weakness of
those people who have wronged me, and give me
the grace to forgive them from my heart.
—Amen.

for · give · ness

gen·er·a·tion, noun.

1. a group of individuals living at the same time.
2. a single step in the line of descent.
3. a period of time defined by the lifestyles of a given age group.
4. **Biblical:** the time and age group in which one lives.
5. **Personal:** the people you are born among.

gen·er·a·tion

God's plan is clear. Children are intended to be a sacred trust, a heritage from the Lord. They are to be cherished, taught, and equipped to live heroic lives. Each generation is to prepare the next generation to serve the Lord.

This was God's plan. Every generation fulfills its destiny by investing in the destiny of the next generation. What a world it would have made! But something stood in the way. Something crept in that made some generations turn inward and fail their obligation to their children.

You can see this force operating in the life of King Hezekiah. In 2 Kings 20, King Hezekiah had sinned by showing the treasures of his kingdom to Babylonian emissaries. This act displeased the Lord, and Isaiah the prophet told Hezekiah the judgment that would befall him. Everything he had would be carried off into captivity, Isaiah said. What is more, "your descendents, your own flesh

After David had served his generation according to the will of God, he died and was buried, and his body decayed.
Acts 13:36 NLT

words
to live by

and blood, that will be born to you, will be taken away, and they will become eunuchs in the palace of the king of Babylon" (v. 18 NIV).

It was horrible; the worst kind of destruction. Not only would all that King Hezekiah had received in trust from previous generations be destroyed but so would everything he had built up during his reign. Most terrible of all, his children would never give Hezekiah grandchildren but would serve foreign rulers and foreign gods in a foreign land. Hezekiah and the generations that should have come from him were to be no more.

The most astonishing part of this story is Hezekiah's response. He did not fall to the ground in grief. He did not sit in sackcloth and ashes. He did not cry out to God for mercy. Instead, he said calmly to Isaiah, "The word you have spoken is good." It is a strange statement, but then Scripture reveals what Hezekiah was thinking: "Will I not have peace and safety in my lifetime?"

With these words, Hezekiah defined the attitude that has kept untold generations from fulfilling their destiny. When one generation becomes more concerned with its own peace and safety than it is concerned with preparing the next generation for its calling, the progress of the kingdom is slowed. Fathers and sons disconnect, heritage is not transferred, and each generation finds itself in worse shape than the generation that went before.

It is a haunting vision. In fact, Scripture describes this condition with one word: *cursed*.

> Each generation wastes a little more of the future with greed and lust for riches.
> **DONALD ROBERT PERRY MARQUIS**

ness grace mercy love faith goodness truth freedom hope
orgiveness peace humble holiness obey repent perfect submit
serve fellowship comforter transformed noble character church

Breaking the Curse

In the last verse of the Old Testament, Malachi said that the Messiah would come and turn the hearts of the children to the fathers or else he would "come and strike the land with a curse." This is what a "generation gap" is, a curse. This is what it means when the parents no longer care for the well-being of their children's generation. It is a curse.

Yet notice the beginning of that last verse in the Old Testament. Among everything else the Messiah came to do, he came to mend the disconnect between generations. He came to heal the hearts of the generations. Now the fathers invest, the sons receive, and the kingdom advances. The curse is lifted as a glorious, God-fearing culture is transmitted from generation to generation.

The Lord is good: his mercy is everlasting; and his truth endures to all generations.
Psalm 100:5 MKJV

❶

How do you help to fulfill this generational calling on your age? You realize, first of all, that a generational calling exists, and that you are part of an age God has destined for specific purposes. Second, you repent of your preoccupation with what Francis Schaeffer called "personal peace and affluence." Third, you start living to launch the next generation. This is how each generation fulfills its purpose in God.

words
to live by

Things you might not know about *generation:*

❶ According to Scripture, the worst thing that can happen to a person after death is for his memory to be wiped out. The Bible presents the success of one generation as being measured in the next generation, while the person who is cursed has his memory cut off for all generations.

❶ Disregard for one's children is classified as a sign of mental illness. Parents who exhibit such traits are charged with crimes, lose authority over their children, and, in some countries, are forbidden to have more children. As it is with an individual, so it is with a generation.

A revolution only lasts fifteen years, a period which coincides with the effectiveness of a generation.
JOSE ORTEGA Y GASSET

Each generation is the gift of their parents to the future.
HAROLD PAUL

What the LORD has planned will stand forever. His thoughts never change.
Psalm 33:11 CEV

God, turn my heart to my sons and daughters. Let me so live as to prepare them for the battles of their time and to launch them into the purposes of God. Cleanse me of generational selfishness, break the thinking of a Hezekiah in my life, and let me depart knowing I have done your will in my time.
—Amen.

gen·er·a·tion

Your Meaning and Your Dream

God, noun.

1. the supreme or ultimate reality.
2. the perfect Being who is worshiped as creator and ruler of the universe.
3. (l.c.) one controlling a particular aspect or part of reality.
4. **Biblical:** the Maker of heaven and earth, Father of the Lord Jesus Christ.
5. **Personal:** the One who made you, saves you, and calls you.

G o d

God is one, and there is no other besides Him.
Mark 12:32 MKJV

words
to live by

This is a secular age, or so modern people are told. No longer do people believe in God. Religion has been proven a mere psychological crutch, and now a more scientific age prevails. God doesn't exist. He never did. Or as one publication said in headlines of the 1960s, "God is dead."

Yet it is strange that human beings can't seem to let God go. Just let a big enough crisis arise, and people who had called themselves atheists immediately start praying, talking about God, and hoping for his mercy. So why is it that humankind can't wash the idea of God out of its consciousness once and for all?

The Christian knows. It is because God exists, and he won't be quiet. He keeps speaking of himself, especially to those who don't want to listen.

People can't seem to stop holding on to God because people are made in the image of God. As Ecclesiastes 3:11 says, "He has put eternity in [our] hearts" (NKJV). People have a part of themselves that keep speaking of another world, that keeps drawing their souls toward a Creator. The voice is too loud and the drive to know a higher being too strong to deny. God seems near, even to atheists in crisis.

Humankind also can't seem to deny God because God is ever speaking through his creation. Romans 1 says that the creation so reveals God that the nonbeliever is without excuse. God's qualities—his eternal power and divine nature—are undeniable even to atheists because nature speaks of them. Psalm 19 even says that the heavens "pour forth speech" constantly. So it is with all of creation.

This explains why even those who talk like they don't believe in God usually believe in "something," some higher power or greater being. And this also explains why humankind left to itself doesn't arrive at atheism. It arrives, instead, at a belief in God. No explorer has ever discovered a primitive tribe that had no religion. Every tribe has a concept of god, and every tribe has a religion until some supposedly advanced and civilized theory convinces people that no God exists.

What does this mean to those who believe? It means that the God Christians

> God is that, the greater than which cannot be conceived.
> **SAINT ANSELM**

Your Meaning and Your Dream

In Him we live and move and have our being, as also certain of your own poets have said, For we are also His offspring.
Acts 17:28 MKJV

worship is larger than their own experience. He has made the universe and he speaks through it, reaching constantly to those who don't acknowledge him as well as to those who do. He is a God who wants to be known, intimately. He isn't happy if people simply say that he exists. He wants to be understood. He has taken great pains to reveal himself and make his nature known. Christians worship him, in part, by knowing him and by drawing the attention of the nonbeliever to all the ways that he is speaking to them.

It moves the heart to worship a God who has done so much to make himself known to humankind. He is not the god of Deism, the religion that says that God started the world but isn't involved in it. Instead, the Christian God has used the world to call his creatures to a relationship with him. Christians worship him, then, by responding to his call and drawing others to do the same.

words
to live by

Things you might not know about *God:*

❶ A recent *U.S. News & World Report* study shed some important light on the state of religion in America. The study revealed that some four in five Americans believe in the existence of God and believe that they have experienced his presence at least once in their lives.

❶ Interestingly, belief in God seems to be connected to happiness. A recent survey showed that people who affirm a belief in God tend to report a greater sense of well-being and life satisfaction than those who can attest to no belief in God.

God is more truly imagined than expressed, and he exists more truly than he is imagined.
SAINT AUGUSTINE OF HIPPO

Live near to God, and so all things will appear to you little in comparison with eternal realities.
ROBERT M. MCCHEYNE

It is a fearful thing to fall into the hands of the living God
Hebrews 10:31 MKJV

God, you have gone to such great lengths to reveal yourself and invite humankind into relationship with you. Help me respond, grant me a spirit of wisdom and revelation to know you, and draw near to me as I draw near to you.
—Amen.

God

97

heal, verb.

1. to make sound or whole.
2. to cause (an undesirable condition) to be overcome.
3. to restore to original purity or integrity.
4. **Biblical:** to make whole.
5. **Personal:** to restore you to your intended condition.

heal

The story is a revelation of Jesus as a healer. It is tender. It is thrilling. And it reveals that healing is about more than just the human body.

Luke 17 tells the moving tale of the Ten Lepers. Understanding this moment in Jesus' life means first understanding the horror that leprosy was in the ancient world. The ancient world knew no cure for leprosy. The very mention of it evoked terror. The disease ate away at the flesh, usually around the head and face, leaving great swaths of raw flesh. When men or women contracted this dreaded condition, they were removed from the community. They were required to grow their hair long and leave their clothes unkempt. If they spoke, they were required to cover their upper lip and, if anyone approached, they were made to shout, "Unclean, unclean."

For everything there is a season, and a time for every matter under heaven . . . a time to heal.
Ecclesiastes 3:1, 3
NRSV

Hard as you might try to imagine it, you cannot do justice to the suffering of a leper. Imagine being separated from children, parents, and community. Imagine being regarded with fear, even by your dearest friends. Picture the corrosive loneliness, the agonizing sense that you are cursed by God, and the hollowness of knowing that the unfolding years of your life offer no deliverance from the cycles of your suffering.

This was the life of the ten lepers who lived near a village on the border between Samaria and Galilee. Yet on the day that is described in Luke 17, they had an unfamiliar hope awaken in their hearts. They had heard that a man was in the nearby village, a man named Jesus. He was known for removing the sicknesses of people just like them. Perhaps he would have mercy on them too.

The ten lepers talked among themselves, made their decision, and approached the village. People were horrified when they saw the ten coming, and the lepers must have wondered if they would be driven off with stones and curses. Then they saw Jesus. They knew they couldn't draw closer, and they wouldn't have infected him for the world, but they needed to try to reach him. Shouting as loudly as their weakened bodies allowed, they shouted, "Jesus, Master, have pity." Jesus saw them and responded simply: "Go, show yourselves to the priests." They turned, they ran, and they were healed. The raw flesh, the stench, the eroded ears and noses—they were made new.

God helps the sick in two ways, through the science of medicine and surgery and through the science of faith and prayer.
NORMAN VINCENT PEALE

less grace mercy love faith goodness truth freedom hope
orgiveness peace humble holiness obey repent perfect submit
serve fellowship comforter transformed noble character church

> He himself bore our sins in his body on the cross, so that, free from sins, we might live for righteousness; by his wounds you have been healed.
> I Peter 2:24 NRSV

While the others rejoiced, one leper couldn't help himself. He turned, ran to Jesus, fell at his feet, and worshiped him. For a leper, this was not allowed. But this man knew he was healed, a leper no more. Jesus said simply, "Rise and go, your faith has made you well." All the lepers had been healed, but this tenth leper was "made whole." It means that the ruts in his soul, the agonies of his heart, were removed along with the ravaged flesh.

In Luke 17, Jesus taught, as usual, by his actions: He can heal your body and he can heal your souls. It is the same to him, and he desires to do both. All you must do is ask him, act on his commands, and then worship him for his mercy. He is the healer, and he makes both the inner and the outer being whole.

words
to live by

Things you might not know about *healing:*

❶ Jesus placed priority on relieving the distress of people. A simple scan of the Gospels reveals that Jesus healed the sick more than he performed any other miracle during his earthly ministry.

❶ In the Western world, where medicine is so readily available, physical suffering is not as central to the human experience. This is not so in most of the world. It is estimated that nearly twenty percent of the human race are seriously ill at any given moment.

God heals and the doctor takes the fee.
BENJAMIN FRANKLIN

Miracles may be denied, but healings are not. . . . Christ produces a sound faith, and faith has a therapeutic value.
JOHN J. GERSTNER

When Jesus had called the Twelve together, he gave them power and authority to drive out all demons and to cure diseases.
Luke 9:1 NIV

heal

God, heal me. Heal both my inner and outer being that I might be a trophy of your grace and free to do your will in the world.
—Amen.

heav·en, noun.

1. the expanse that seems to be over the earth like a dome.
2. a spiritual state of everlasting communion with God.
3. a place or condition of utmost happiness.
4. **Biblical:** the timeless realm in which God dwells.
5. **Personal:** the place that is ultimately your home.

heav·en

Jesus said to him, "If you wish to be complete, go and sell your possessions and give to the poor, and you shall have treasure in heaven; and come, follow Me."
Matthew 19:21 NASB

You are told in the Bible that your citizenship is in heaven, that you are seated in heavenly places with Christ Jesus, and that in this life you will always long for your heavenly dwellings.

Strangely, though, the Bible doesn't tell you what heaven is.

Oh, you are told about heaven. The Bible tells you that heaven is where God dwells, where the angels work, and where the Spirit comes from. You find out that Jesus came from heaven, that he "passed through the heavens" when he ascended, and that he is on the right hand of God in heaven now.

You know that Paul was caught up into the third heaven, that the heavens sometimes open, that the windows of heaven open up to allow blessing on God's people. You know also that you possess every spiritual blessing in heavenly places, that spirits of wickedness exist in heaven-

words
to live by

ly places, as does a heavenly tabernacle that is the glorious original of all the earthly ones. Those earthly tabernacles reveal how God is enthroned in heaven, where Jesus had to cleanse the heavenly utensils of heavenly worship, and how God rules from heaven.

In the Bible, people pray to heaven, look to heaven, cry out to heaven, and hope for heaven. You are told to store up your treasures in heaven, that in heaven you won't be getting married, and that you have mansions being prepared for you in heaven.

To really confuse the matter, one day the heavens won't exist anymore. The Bible reports that heaven and earth are going to pass away and that one day new ones will appear. Apparently, even God needs to remodel from time to time.

You are obviously told a great deal about heaven, but you aren't ever told what, exactly, it is, where it is, or what it looks like. You read in the book of Revelation about streets of gold and astonishing beauty, but you aren't quite sure where all that is.

What this means, of course, is that God has told you what you need to know and no more. He often does this. The Bible isn't an exhaustive manual for running the universe. The Bible is what humans need to know to live with God. Apparently, God revealed everything humankind needs to know about heaven for now.

He who thinks most of heaven will do most for earth.
AUTHOR UNKNOWN

uniless grace mercy love faith goodness truth freedom hope
orgiveness peace humble holiness obey repent perfect submit
erve fellowship comforter transformed noble character church

The Home of Your King

> Heaven is my throne, and the earth is my footstool.
>
> Isaiah 66:1 NIV

The most important thing about heaven is this: It is where you belong. Whatever assignments you have on earth, heaven is where you are anchored, the point from which you view life, your destination, and the place you best fit. This transforms your life in this world. You aren't supposed to fit perfectly here. You are on a holy mission. You can relax, be the pilgrim and stranger you have to be in this life, and even more energetically do the good you are called to do.

Heaven is where you will live forever after this life. It is there, waiting for you. With that confidence, and the trust that God is looking down from heaven now to give you every resource you need, you can take hold of that for which Christ Jesus has taken hold of you. As the Bible says, you are a citizen of heaven. Here, you are a foreign worker under assignment from your King.

words
to live by

Things you might not know about *heaven:*

● Hebrews tells about a source of inspiration for living in this life, and it says that the saints of old are in heaven watching lives on earth and that by remembering them you can be energized by their example.

● It is noted by philosophers that every religion and human ideology has some concept of heaven, of an ideal state. The need for the existence of a perfect state seems to be hard-wired into the soul of humankind.

Heaven is not to be looked upon only as the reward, but as the natural effect, of a religious life.
JOSEPH ADDISON

Things learned on earth, we shall practice in heaven.
ROBERT BROWNING

He must remain in heaven until the time for the final restoration of all things, as God promised long ago through his prophets.
Acts 3:21 NLT

God, anchor my consciousness in heaven, grant me the resources of heaven, and cause me to live for the applause of heaven.
—Amen.

h e a v · e n

he·ro, *noun.*

1. the central figure in an event, period, or movement.
2. an illustrious warrior.
3. one who shows great courage.
4. **Biblical:** one who breaks through barriers for the sake of others.
5. **Personal:** the bold and courageous whom we emulate and seek to become.

he·ro

See now, the Lord,
the LORD Almighty, is
about to take from
Jerusalem and Judah
. . . the hero.
Isaiah 3:1–2 NIV

When you ask people today who their heroes are, you get very revealing answers. If you listen closely, you will find that the people they celebrate as heroes are merely the famous and the talented. The fact that they are included in a list of heroes really has little to do with what "kind" of people they are or what good they do for others. They are merely well known, talented, or rich.

The word *hero* is used frequently in the Bible. It is sometimes translated "mighty man" or "mighty warrior," but the word is close to what people mean by the word *hero* today. It is an important word in the Bible. In fact, it is used over 130 times. Yet it is used in the Bible in a way that is a bit different from the modern word for *hero*, and Christians desperately need to understand this greater biblical meaning.

In the Bible, a hero is someone who

God's Barrier Busters

words
to live by

lives in such a way as to break through barriers so that others can rise to their best, to their destiny. Heroes in the biblical view change the boundaries, redefine the battles, and achieve victories so that others can rise to even greater heights. These heroes might defeat a vicious enemy or occupy new territory; they might reach some greater depth in God or even overcome some area of bondage in their own lives.

A good example of this heroic principle comes from the world of sports. For centuries, no one had ever broken the four-minute mile. Men spoke of this barrier with reverence and wondered if it would ever be surpassed. Then in 1954 an Oxford medical student by the name of Roger Bannister taught himself to train in new ways, and on May 6, 1954, he ran the mile in less than four minutes. The news electrified people around the world.

Now, you would expect that no one would have broken the four-minute mile for quite some time afterward. In fact, some at the time wondered if it would ever be done again. Yet just six weeks after Roger Bannister broke this historic record, another man on another continent ran the mile in less than four minutes. The world was astonished, and even more so when within a few years some half a dozen men had broken the once unbreakable record. Somehow Roger Bannister made it possible for human beings he had never met to do what they could never have done without him.

There is no social transformation without heroes. The hero shows the people what may be accomplished, leaving them to live as they once thought impossible.

ABRAHAM JEHUDA

God's Barrier Busters

They said to one another, "Look, here comes the hero of those dreams! Let's kill him."
Genesis 37:19–20
CEV

This is the heroic principle as taught in the Bible. Heroes are not just the famous and the talented. They are the ones who live so as to make a greater kind of life possible for others. A hero is the father who decides that the family history of alcoholism is going to stop in his generation. A hero is the mother who determines that anger is not going to be passed down her family line to her children. A hero is the church that decides their community's history of racism has to stop in their day. And yes, a hero is the person who charged into a burning building on September 11, 2001, so that people they had never met could live.

The biblical call to a heroic life is not just for the famous, the rich, or the talented. It is for all who are willing to live beyond the barriers that have kept them from their best. Now the question you have to ask yourself is, "What are the barriers I am called to punch through so that my children and my children's children can arise to their destiny?" This is the question heroes ask themselves before their day of greatness.

words
to live by

Things you might not know about *hero:*

❶ There is a theory of the heroic often pondered by sociologists. Apparently, heroes are essential to the process of social change. Because heroes embody and symbolize new ways of living, because they display new possibilities, they provide both hope and a pathway for society as a whole.

❶ People live their lives empowered by a model of the ideal life that they carry in their heads. This ideal life is largely the result of the heroes they have acquired throughout their lives.

Neither the king nor the warrior can be depended upon to save the country, and so our only hope lies in grass-roots heroes.
YOSHIDA SHOIN

Heroes are not the ones that never fail, but the ones who never give up.
AUTHOR UNKNOWN

Controlling your temper is better than being a hero who captures a city.
Proverbs 16:32 CEV

God, do not let me live as a mere man or a mere woman.
Do not let me pass on to the next generation what has
bested those before me. Let me break through barriers—
of my soul, of my family, of my nation—to leave a better
life for those after me. Let me live the heroic life that
Jesus models and calls me to.
—Amen.

h e • r o

free grace mercy love faith goodness truth freedom hope
rgiveness peace humble holiness obey repent perfect submit
erve fellowship comforter transformed noble character church

ho·li·ness, noun.

1. the state of being morally pure.
2. freedom from sin.
3. the state of anything hallowed or consecrated to God.
4. **Biblical:** the condition of being set apart for God.
5. **Personal:** the virtue of life lived for God and not for the world.

ho·li·ness

God has made us these promises. So we should stay away from everything that keeps our bodies and spirits from being clean. We should honor God and try to be completely like him.

2 Corinthians 7:1 CEV

For thousands of years, Christians have wrestled with the question of holiness. How do believers in Jesus live out the character of Jesus and avoid the river of this world's moral sewage? Do they separate physically from the world, as Christian hermits have done for centuries? Do they adopt codes of conduct and dress that assure separation from carnal ways? Or do they welcome as much of the world as possible without crossing the most basic standards of Christian morality?

It isn't an easy question. How are Christians to be in the world but not of it? And the question is even more pressing since the Bible says that friendship with the world is opposition to God, and that without holiness no one will see God.

The Greek word for *holiness* means to be separate or apart from something. Clearly, God calls believers to make a dis-

words
to live by

tinction between themselves and their former "root system" in the world. Believers aren't to have the same values or center their lives around the same desires as nonbelievers when it comes to how they conduct themselves.

The problem with holiness for most Christians is that it becomes about what they aren't to do rather than who they are to be about. Holiness isn't simply an ethical system. Holiness is the change Christians undergo as they grow toward God.

When a man and a woman marry, they enter into a process of change. It is natural. They have committed themselves to live their lives in terms of the other. Their focus is upon becoming what they need to become to make the other happy and to make the marriage the beautiful thing it can be. Habits fall off, social arrangements change, time priorities realign, and the ultimate concerns of life transform to fit both the passion and the commitment of their hearts. This is all the natural product of devotion.

It is the same way in your relationship with God. Once you devote yourself to knowing Jesus and doing his will, your life begins a process of transformation much like the newly married. You too are growing toward a person. You too are allowing your life to be radically altered to please the object of your affection, Jesus Christ.

This process, though people seldom think of it this way, is really the process of holiness. Christians live differently from the

A holy life is a voice; it speaks when the tongue is silent, and is either a constant attraction or a perpetual reproof.
ROBERT LEIGHTON

unless grace mercy love faith goodness truth freedom hope
orgiveness peace humble holiness obey repent perfect submit
serve fellowship comforter transformed noble character church

A Life After God

people of this world because they are given to a different love. This passion for Jesus pulls them in a different direction, reforms their desires, revises their ethics, and reworks the basic desires that shape their lives.

But this isn't just a discipline. It is a love affair. You don't stop cussing or being entertained by the impure just because a religious legal system demands it. You change in these areas because you are allowing yourself to be fitted for a relationship. You aren't trying just to be holy; you are trying to be for the Holy One. There is a difference. The one approach produces pressure, fear, and failure. The other is joy and the abandoning of this world's ways for a lover from a far different place.

Take a moment to ask yourself if your approach to holiness has been fueled by a passionate love for Jesus or by a nervous fear of breaking "the rules." Many Christians find themselves fighting battles for purity that are really battles for love of Jesus. The truth is, low spiritual passion usually means low holiness and purity. The issue is not rules. The issue is fueling the fires of passion for the glorious Son of God.

words
to live by

Things you might not know about *holiness:*

❶ Among the desires older people expressed in a recent survey as they reviewed their lives was that they could feel "innocent" again. This is simply a longing for what the Christian calls holiness.

❶ The fastest growing cults in America get most of their converts from the pews of Christian churches. The reason: Those new converts perceive the cults as possessing greater moral purity than the churches in which they were converted.

Holiness is the symmetry of the soul.
PHILIP HENRY

It is a great deal better to live a holy life than to talk about it. Lighthouses do not ring bells and fire cannon to call attention to their shining—they just shine.
DWIGHT L. MOODY

Christ Jesus . . . who through the Spirit of holiness was declared with power to be the Son of God.
Romans 1:1, 4 NIV

God, forgive me for pursuing holiness without pursuing Jesus. Lead me in the holiness that lets me see you, please you, and be useful to you.
—Amen.

h · o · l · i · n · e · s · s

hos·pi·tal·i·ty, noun.

1. the entertaining of strangers without reward.
2. the act of readily receiving guests.
3. the offer of a pleasant or sustaining environment.
4. **Biblical:** the love of strangers.
5. **Personal:** your life and home offered to the service of God.

h o s · p i · t a l · i · t y

Hospitality has received a great deal of attention in this generation. As the developed portions of the world have experienced unparalleled prosperity, people have begun thinking about their homes, their social gatherings, their manners, and their "style" more than ever. Hospitality has become about how to give a party, how to decorate a home, and how to anticipate the needs of others. Magazines, Web sites, television shows, and famous experts all help people do "hospitality with grace."

This is, perhaps, as it should be. Beauty, manners, and social gatherings are all important in life, and there is no reason not to learn how to do them well. In an age when social graces are rarely handed down from generation to generation, it is natural that books and television would step in to fill the void once filled by parents. A problem arises for the Christian, though, and that is that he will confuse

Share with God's people who are in need. Practice hospitality.
Romans 12:13 NIV

Showing Love for Strangers

<u>words</u>
to live by

hospitality as a style with the biblical emphasis on hospitality as a ministry.

The biblical word for *hospitality* has little to do with style and decorating. In Greek, the word is *philoxenia*. It literally means "love for strangers." As important as tending friends and family is, the biblical concept of hospitality is that Christians show kindness for people they don't know. It is an important distinction to make because the kingdom of God grows on the strength of hospitality.

Jesus' entire ministry on earth was dependent upon hospitality from the manger in which he was born to the homes in which he stayed. Paul also depended upon the hospitality of believers and even commanded Philemon to prepare a room for him to stay in as though part of Philemon's duty was to provide hospitality for God's leaders. All throughout the New Testament, you find people being fed, housed, churched, and ministered to in the homes and from the resources of people they didn't know.

In fact, hospitality is very much at the center of the message of Jesus. He talked about having banquets for people who were brought in from the streets. He preached of taking the poor into homes, of giving to those who asked for help, and he even taught that kindness for the needy and for prisoners was kindness to him.

> A tree is known by its fruit; a man by his deeds. A good deed is never lost; he who sows courtesy reaps friendship, and he who plants kindness gathers love.
> **SAINT BASIL**

Hospitality in its true form is demonstration of the

dness grace mercy love faith goodness truth freedom hope
orgiveness peace humble holiness obey repent perfect submit
serve fellowship comforter transformed noble character church

Showing Love for Strangers

> Do not neglect to show hospitality to strangers, for by doing that some have entertained angels without knowing it.
>
> **Hebrews 13:2** NRSV

love of God. When you show kindness to someone you do not know and cannot benefit from, you model the unmerited favor of God in Jesus. You give what is not deserved because you love, just as God gave you what you do not deserve because he loved. This is hospitality, to meet the needs of strangers in the name of Jesus and asking nothing in return.

❶

Imagine how the border of the kingdom of God would expand if Christians began to systematically practice love for strangers. How might the people of the world see the gospel message afresh if Christians they did not know showed them more love than non-Christians they do know? It might change their lives. Even if it didn't, Jesus would take it as though you were showing him kindness. Besides, Hebrews 13:2 says that you might be entertaining angels. Now that's a party!

words
to live by

Things you might not know about *hospitality:*

1 A church historian has said that many of the social institutions we have today began with the simple opening of a Christian home to tend the needs of strangers; hospitals, orphanages, mental institutions, schools, and hospices are some examples.

1 At a time when Christians in America are not making enough converts to keep up with the birth rates, it is interesting to note why people turn to other faiths. New converts to Islam cite Middle Eastern practices of hospitality as one of the primary reasons for their conversion.

A little kindness from person to person is better than a vast love for all humankind.
RICHARD DEHMEL

True religion is measured in hospitality.
MOTHER TERESA

A bishop must be above reproach, married only once, temperate, sensible, respectable, hospitable.
I Timothy 3:2 NRSV

God, take my home, my property, my time, my skills.
Infuse them with your love that I might reach those I do
not know in your name.
—Amen.

h·o·s·p·i·t·a·l·i·t·y

The Path to Power

hum·ble, verb.

1. to reduce to a low state.
2. to lack signs of pride.
3. to reduce arrogance and self-dependence.
4. **Biblical:** to have lowliness of mind borne of utter dependence on God.
5. **Personal:** to see yourself as small in your own eyes.

h u m · b l e

Humble yourselves therefore under the mighty hand of God, so that he may exalt you in due time.

1 Peter 5:6 NRSV

In the city of humankind, powerful people command the obedience of others. In the city of God, the one who would be powerful must serve others. In the city of humankind, the low are ground underfoot. In the city of God, the humble are exalted by a merciful God. In the city of humankind, ambition rules. In the city of God, meekness rules. The kingdom of God is what some have called "the upside-down kingdom."

This understanding of God's kingdom reveals how humility is the path to power. The word *humble* means "to be voluntarily low." It means that a believer conquers ambition and understands that the low, the meek, and the quiet are what God chooses to use in his kingdom.

This humility, though, is not rooted in insecurity or fear. It is actually the fruit of power. Because Christians know that they have the guarantees of God, because

words
to live by

they know that they do not craft their own lives, they can rest from the pressure of ambition and of making their own way. They can choose to be at peace, to live at their natural level. And they can afford to tend the small and the unnoticed because they are unconcerned with orchestrating their own life's path.

Such Christians also walk in humility because they have experienced the power of salvation. They know what they were apart from grace. The great nineteenth-century evangelist Dwight Moody was walking down a street when his companion pointed with disgust to a man who was drunk. Moody watched the man for a moment and said, "There, there I am but for the grace of God."

Moody knew what the true Christian knows: He is nothing apart from God's grace. Humility, then, isn't an act. It is living near to the truth. Humble Christians don't have to convince themselves that they are nothing apart from God. They know they are and live accordingly. Humble Christians don't put on humility as a cloak. Their humility issues from the heart because it is the fruit of the truth.

But the humble Christian has also learned how the kingdom of God works. They know the truth from the book of Jonah, that those who cling to worthless idols forfeit the grace that could be theirs. They know that self is an idol they must pull down in order to be of use to their God. They have seen the society that people have

Many would be scantily clad if clothed in their humility.
Author Unknown

uriess grace mercy love faith goodness truth freedom hope
orgiveness peace humble holiness obey repent perfect submit
serve fellowship comforter transformed noble character church

The Path to Power

built. It doesn't work. They want to be useful to their God, and they know that humility is the price. God's kingdom is led by the servants, by the broken believer God has fixed, and by the small in their own eyes. The one who wants to be of impact knows he must "get low" in order to "get useful" in God's hands.

Humility is not being a doormat. It is not forgoing all strength and skill. Instead, it is knowing who you are, whom you belong to, and who you are called to be. It is resting from your own efforts to achieve and relying on God to advance you. It is also understanding the kingdom of God and the peace to which God has called his people.

> Whoever shall exalt himself shall be abased, and he who shall humble himself shall be exalted.
> Matthew 23:12 MKJV

To walk in humility, first repent of your striving and your preoccupation with image. Place your life afresh in God's hands and trust that he is the "Destiny Maker." He will make you what you are called to be, and your efforts to stage-manage or artificially prop up won't make any difference. Rest from your striving is possible, but it is the rest only of those willing to get small in God's hands in order to be great in God's purposes.

words
to live by

etcetera . . .

Things you might not know about *humble:*

❶ A wise man once said that only the humble are free enough from self to see who they really are.

❶ Humility is an attitude. To humble oneself is a course of practical action. To be humble is to do the deeds of humility on a constant basis.

It is from out of the depths of our humility that the height of our destiny looks grandest. Let me truly feel that in myself I am nothing, and at once, through every inlet of my soul, God comes in, and is everything in me.
WILLIAM MOUNTFORD

He leads the humble in what is right, and teaches the humble his way.
Psalm 25:9 NRSV

True humility is contentment
HENRI FREDERIC AMIEL

God, even as Jesus was humble and so accomplished your will, so I yearn to be freed of self and filled with a faith that my life, my reputation, and my destiny are in your hands. Grant me to be small that I might be great.
—Amen.

h u m · b l e

knowl·edge, noun.

1. the sum of what is known.
2. the body of truth, information, and principles acquired by humankind.
3. a branch of learning.
4. **Biblical:** the understanding of the truth of God.
5. **Personal:** the truth that you master and live.

k n o w l · e d g e

In him lie hidden all the treasures of wisdom and knowledge.
Colossians 2:3 NLT

The Bible seems to suggest that knowledge is not good for you. Ecclesiastes says that "of the making of books there is no end and much study is a weariness to the bones." In another place, the Bible says that "knowledge puffs up but love edifies." That statement alone would seem to be enough to douse the lamp of knowledge. There is even a figure in the Bible who is told that his great amount of learning has made him crazy. No wonder some Christians have believed that if you get learnin' you'll lose your burnin' for God.

Yet Christians are constantly commanded to study, to meditate, and to learn. Proverbs says that it is the glory of God to conceal a matter and the glory of kings to search it out. This is not to mention that just reading the Bible moved Western civilization more toward scholarship and knowledge than any other single

words
to live by

source. Consider the fields of knowledge the Bible requires to know it fully: three ancient languages, geography, the history of dozens of civilizations, poetry, literature, psychology, economics, and, of course, theology and comparative religions. Clearly, biblical religion is not a religion that countenances ignorance.

So how do you balance these two seemingly contradictory emphases in Scripture? How do you reconcile the cautions about knowledge with the demand for knowledge in the Bible?

It seems that what God is getting at is not so much knowledge versus ignorance, but rather knowledge in the right perspective. Throughout history, people have believed that knowledge is power, knowledge is salvation, and knowledge is the blessing of the righteous only. None of these beliefs is true. Instead, what God seems to require is knowledge in the right perspective.

Clearly, for Christians, all knowledge is God's knowledge. Everything true belongs to God. There is no mathematical formula or truth of psychology or medical certainty that God did not create. Nor is he apart from history, law, or economics. It is all God's, all created by him, and all of it reveals his thinking and wisdom. In fact, it could be said that to study is, in a sense, to seek after God, for all truth derived by study is a revelation of who he is.

All knowledge and wonder, which is the seed of knowledge, is an impression of pleasure in itself.
FRANCIS BACON

This is the perspective God calls his people to. The goal is never knowledge for

ness grace mercy love faith goodness truth freedom hope
orgiveness peace humble holiness obey repent perfect submit
serve fellowship comforter transformed noble character church

Thinking the Thoughts of God

its own sake or for the sake of ego and power. Rather, it is knowledge viewed in light of a Creator. This is what the psalmist meant by "in your light we see light." The Christian is called to understand all truth as God's truth, to view the world through the understanding that everything was made by God and everything serves his purposes.

The glory of this way of thinking is revealed in the great Christian intellectual achievements of history. From the great universities of the world to major scientific achievements, to accomplishments as diverse as great literature and break-through surgery, the Christian passion to know the world as God has made it has fueled the engine of human progress.

His divine power has given us every-thing needed for life and godliness, through the knowl-edge of him who called us by his own glory and goodness.
2 Peter 1:3 NRSV

Knowledge in the light of God is a bless-ing, a gift, a tool, and a revelation. Believers aren't warned about knowing. They are warned about making an idol of knowledge apart from God. Once you understand this distinction, you can use your mind to the glory of God and honor him by knowing him through his works.

words
to live by

Things you might not know about *knowledge:*

1 Do you ever think that there is just too much to know about in our world? Consider this: In the middle ages, the amount of knowledge the average person would acquire in a lifetime is equal to one Sunday edition of the *New York Times* today.

1 The modern world experiences a revolution in knowledge every thirty-six months. This means that what a college student learns his first year of college may well be obsolete by his last year in college.

Consider your origin; you were not born to live like brutes, but to follow virtue and knowledge.
DANTE ALIGHIERI

Knowledge is power.
FRANCIS BACON

Always learning and never able to come to the knowledge of the truth.
2 Timothy 3:7 NASB

God, thank you for the joy of knowledge, of thinking your thoughts after you, and of seeing you revealed in what you have made. Teach me and let me be useful in this information age in which you have called me to live.
—Amen.

k n o w l · e d g e

More Than Merely Free

lib·er·ty, noun.

1. the power to do as one pleases.
2. the freedom from arbitrary or despotic control.
3. the possibility of choice.
4. **Biblical:** the release from bondage and constraint.
5. **Personal:** your emergence from the old self to the new.

lib·er·ty

A great deal is said of liberty in the Western world. It seems to be what humans seek, what governments are supposed to assure, and what humankind strives to achieve in almost every realm of life. Liberty is the goal, the Mecca, the New Jerusalem of a generation's dreams, and the measure of well-being.

I will walk at liberty: for I seek thy precepts.
Psalm 119:45 KJV

Yet most people have only a vague notion of what liberty is. For some it is doing whatever they want. For others it is complete freedom from authority. For many it is living as they wish without consequence.

The problem is, liberty can be a curse as much as a blessing. Humans were not made to be free just to be free. They were made to be free to serve a higher purpose. When a secular society exalts liberty to near religious status but offers no purpose for that liberty, it sets up its citizens for a horrible fate. As one philosopher has said, "Freedom can be the loneliest state of all."

words
to live by

His point is that when a people have become free of restraint, free of authority, and free of consequences, they are also in danger of becoming free of meaning, free of community, and free of purpose.

One version of liberty is merely a stripping of everything that defines life. If liberty is freedom from authority, then it may also be freedom from belonging. If liberty is freedom from consequence, then it may also be freedom from morality and religion as well. And if liberty is freedom to do as one pleases without boundaries, then liberty may then be transformed into the perfect definition of isolation. Truly, there is a kind of liberty that is the loneliest existence of all, and this seems to be where Western society is leading. Perhaps this explains why humankind is freer than ever before and yet increasingly unhappy.

The liberty God offers is not a stripping of all that gives life meaning. It is a freeing from the lesser to reach to the higher. It is a destroying of the bondages and the deformities of life to allow God's people to live for him. It is leaving the prison of the kingdom of darkness to serve in the kingdom of God.

Yet it is not a liberty from restraint, authority, or consequence. In fact, it is just the opposite. The one made free in Christ is more accountable, more aware of consequence, and more constrained to a certain course of action than he has ever been. But he has chosen this life. The life he lived before was one of domination and slavery.

In necessary things, unity; in doubtful things, liberty; in all things, charity.
RICHARD BAXTER

More Than Merely Free

The Spirit of the Lord Jehovah is on Me; because the LORD has anointed Me . . . to proclaim liberty.
Isaiah 61:1 MKJV

By becoming a Christian, he has not left belonging, obligation, and penalty. He, knowing that forgiveness reigns, has simply chosen to belong to God, to be obligated to love, and to welcome the penalties of a new kingdom. He is free, not just to be free, but to give himself freely to a new master. His life becomes rich because he discovers that liberty of a secular kind is not a sufficient force to give his life the meaning he was made for.

🔒

Scan your life to see where you strive for a version of liberty that isn't the liberty of God. When you think of "being free," what do you mean? Are the pictures in your mind painted in the brilliant colors of Scripture or are they drawn from the thin slogans of modernism? Answering these questions may well be the first steps toward the freedom that is free indeed.

words
to live by

Things you might not know about *liberty:*

❶ Few men in world history were as suspicious of liberty as the American Founding Fathers. They were afraid liberty would be wrongly defined and would lead to a society of immorality and license.

❶ The Pilgrim Fathers of America were so concerned about an unrighteous definition of liberty that they once included in a list of sins the tendency toward "extreme liberty."

Those who won our independence believed that the final end of the State was to make men free to develop their faculties; and that in its government the deliberative forces should prevail over the arbitrary. They valued liberty both as an end and as a means. They believed liberty to be the secret of happiness and courage to be the secret of liberty.
LOUIS DEMBITZ BRANDEIS

Whether in chains or in laurels, liberty knows nothing but victories.
WENDELL PHILLIPS

Stand fast therefore in the liberty by which Christ has made us free, and do not be entangled again with a yoke of bondage.
Galatians 5:1 NKJV

God, cleanse me of the view of liberty common in this age and grant me to see that liberty, which comes from being in your presence only.
—Amen.

l i b · e r · t y

ness grace mercy love faith goodness truth freedom hope
orgiveness peace humble holiness obey repent perfect submit
serve fellowship comforter transformed noble character church

Existence as God Meant It

life, noun.

1. the period from birth to death.
2. the quality that distinguishes a vital and functional being from a dead body.
3. a way or manner of living.
4. **Biblical:** a quality of life patterned after and drawn from God.
5. **Personal:** your life lived for God and in his power.

life

Oh, that you would choose life, that you and your descendants might live!
Deuteronomy 30:19
NLT

words
to live by

Without a doubt, some terms used in the English Bible are vastly altered in meaning by even a little understanding of the original Greek language. While English is a magnificent language that is vastly superior for use in many fields, for theological and even poetic expression, English is to Greek as black-and-white movies are to color.

This is particularly true with a word like *life*. In English, there is one word: *life*. It can mean the life of a bee, the life of the party, and the life of a project. It also pertains to every kind of human life, like the life of the mind or the life of the human body. The word has many uses, but its meaning has to be decided by the context. The ancient Greeks used nearly a half a dozen words for *life*, and three of these are particularly important to understanding the Bible.

The first Greek word for life is *bios*.

It pertains to the biological life, the life of the body. However, it is also used to depict the way people conduct themselves, their manner of life. Because the primary meaning of the word is physical, it applies to the things people do: how they move, what they buy, where they go, what they say, and who they are with. This is *bios*—the physical and moral life of believers.

The word that is most often missed because of the use of the English Bible is the word *psuche*. It means the "soul life" or "the psychological life." It describes the seat of the personality: the heart, the mind, and the soul together.

This word is critically important because it is often used in passages where readers might assume the meaning is *bios*. For example, when Jesus says that greater love has no man but that he lays down his life for his friends, the word used is not *bios* but *psuche*. In other words, you must lay down your aspirations, expectations, ways of thinking, and even dreams to give yourself for your friends. This same meaning is intended when Jesus says that if people try to save their lives they will lose them, but that if they want to gain their lives they must lay them down. He is not calling Christians to die physically. He is calling them to surrender their *psuche*, meaning their dreams, ways of thinking, aspirations, hopes, and will. Then, as he gives believers his kind of life, they regain the life they were seeking.

> God asks no man whether he will accept life. That is not the choice. You must accept it. The only choice is how.
> HENRY WARD BEECHER

131

The word that describes life as God has it is *zoe*. This is "life intensive," life in the highest sense. It is a quality of life that is elevated, rich, full, spiritual, yet having a transforming effect on the other kinds of life. *Zoe* is the life God calls his people to, the life Jesus died to give them, and the life they have when they walk in his ways. It is *zoe* that a husband and wife share and which God calls them to protect by their prayers. It is *zoe* that dwells among faithful believers.

In this way they will lay up treasure for themselves as a firm foundation for the coming age, so that they may take hold of the life that is truly life.

1 Timothy 6:19 NIV

These three words for life—"bios," "psuche," and "zoe"—lead to a single conclusion: Jesus has been sent not to renovate the life you have, but to give you a whole new brand of life. This should challenge you. The Christian life is meant to be a different kind of life, a completely alternative force in the world. Perhaps this is where the Greek language serves well: It defines more specifically the uniqueness of what God has made believers to be.

words
to live by

Things you might not know about *life:*

❶ Sometimes the way a word of Greek derivation is used in the English language helps to understand its meaning in the Bible. For example, the Greek word *zoe* is the basis for the English word zoo, a place of intense life.

❷ Scholars of earlier centuries often wrote vast theological tracts on the meaning of Greek words. The results were often interesting. One such scholar wrote, "It is as you walk in holiness of *bios* that you temper your *psuche* which allows for *zoe*."

Be such a man, and live such a life,
That if every man were such as you,
And every life a life like yours,
This earth would be God's Paradise.
PHILLIPS BROOKS

No man is living at his best who is not living at his best spiritually.
W. MARSHALL CRAIG

If you are a husband, you should be thoughtful of your wife. Treat her with honor, because she isn't as strong as you are, and she shares with you in the gift of life.
I Peter 3:7 CEV

God, I desire the life that is truly life. I'm weary of anything less. Teach me your ways, grant me to lay down the willfulness of my soul, and let me know the "God kind of life."
—Amen.

love, noun.

1. a strong affection for another.
2. a warm attachment, enthusiasm, or devotion.
3. an unselfish loyal and benevolent concern for the good of another.
4. **Biblical:** the passion of God for human beings.
5. **Personal:** your obedience to God's commandments toward others.

love

God is love.
1 John 4:8 CEV

words
to live by

It is one of the greatest themes of Christianity, this idea of love. Christians are told that God is love, that love is what put Jesus on the cross, and that believers are supposed to love their neighbors as themselves. In fact, they are supposed to feel such love that they are willing to lay down their lives for one another.

It is thrilling. It is wondrous. And if Christians are honest with themselves, it is a great deal of pressure. In fact, this call to love often means instant guilt for those who take it seriously.

The problem is, people hear this call to love as a call to feel certain things. If the feelings aren't right, then they aren't loving as they should, and the only conclusion left is that they are in sin, hard of heart, and far from God.

It isn't necessarily so. The truth is, people pressure themselves too much.

And they misunderstand Scripture.

Love as the Bible presents it isn't a feeling. Love is a commitment to a course of action that may result in feelings but isn't dependent on feelings. The truth is, many modern ideas about love are recent inventions stemming from the Romantic Movement in literature and music. Romance is wonderful. Romance is God's idea. Yet the kind of love God calls his people to isn't primarily a matter of feeling a certain way toward others. It is a matter of treating people as God commands.

Second John, verse 6, reads, "This is love, that we walk according to His commandments." This is after 1 John 2:5, which reads, "But whoever keeps His Word, truly the love of God is perfected in him" (NKJV). Do you see the emphasis? God doesn't tell you that you are responsible for producing feelings toward people. God tells you that his love flows through your biblical actions toward others.

The fact is, feelings change. They aren't stable, and they usually don't last. If you had a choice between having all your friends "feel good" about you but with the knowledge that their feelings could change, or having all your friends obey Scripture in their treatment of you regardless of their feelings, you would choose the latter. This means your friends would always forgive you, always encourage you, always be generous with you, and, even if they should come one day to view you as an enemy, they would have to bless you because Scripture

Love conquers all.
VIRGIL

135

udness grace mercy love faith goodness truth freedom hope
orgiveness peace humble holiness obey repent perfect submit
erve fellowship comforter transformed noble character church

The Transforming Obedience

> Whoever keeps His word, in him the love of God has truly been perfected. By this we know that we are in Him.
>
> 1 John 2:5 NASB

commands that you bless your enemies. Wouldn't you rather be treated "biblically" even by someone who thinks you are their enemy than to be treated only sentimentally?

This issue of obedience to Scripture is the key to love. Feelings will come, but they follow obedience. You become loving by doing loving things. You become forgiving by forgiving, not by having feelings of forgiveness. You act patiently and a supernatural patience enters your life. Love is the same way. Action first, feeling second.

You can't produce feelings. You can produce action in keeping with the love of God. This is the challenge then: Begin treating the people in your life according to Scripture regardless of feelings. The Bible says that an approach like this will allow love to "run its full course." This is important, for, as Paul says, "Nothing matters except faith working by love."

Things you might not know about *love:*

❶ A poll of people who refused to attend church regularly revealed that those surveyed had tried church but had a common complaint: They found no love in the churches they visited.

❶ Love is universally identified both as the primary need of people and the greatest lack of humankind. As a result, the word *love* occurs in great speeches and poetry more than any other word.

Where love is, there is God also.
LEO TOLSTOY

Whoso loves believes the impossible.
ELIZABETH BARRETT BROWNING

We know how dearly God loves us, because he has given us the Holy Spirit to fill our hearts with his love.
Romans 5:5 NLT

l o v e

God, let your love run its full course in me. Grant me the grace to act lovingly without requiring the feelings of love first. I yearn to love as you love and so complete your work on earth.
—Amen.

man, noun.

1. an individual human
2. an adult male human
3. one possessing in high degree the qualities considered distinctive of manhood
4. *Biblical:* a human created in the masculine image of God
5. *Personal:* the male you are, came from, or hope to be

man

Be strong, show yourself a man, and observe what the LORD your God requires.

I Kings 2:2–3 NIV

You have certainly heard the jokes. A man-eating lion would die of starvation in most churches. There aren't two sexes, there are three: men, women, and preachers. These jibes are humorous ways of making the point that whatever true manhood is, it is hard to find in most Christian churches.

You can be pretty sure you know what people do not mean by manhood. They do not mean the modern archetype of the "macho man." Manhood isn't just a matter of muscle, hair, volume, bravado, or sex appeal. In fact, when the Bible tells a Christian leader that he shouldn't be a striker or a fighter, the word used is the Greek word *macho*. Clearly, manhood isn't about testosterone alone.

You can also be pretty sure that manhood isn't just about a manly style. As much as advertising tries to sell it, a man isn't a man just because he owns a cool car, rides a horse, or smells good. In fact, it is often true that the more a man tries to act like a man in style only, the less he is really a man at heart. Manhood is simply more than manly image.

So what is a man? Clearly David was alluding to some specific qualities when he turned to Solomon from his deathbed and said, "Show yourself a man." He wasn't saying be a male. Solomon was male no matter what he did. David was saying, "Live those characteristics that make a man." In other words, be what a man is: Exhibit the qualities of a man as God has defined them.

Aptitude tests show that women are superior to men in all areas of aptitude except for two: abstract thought and aggression. This may sound like bad news to both genders, but it isn't. Men are made to be the visionaries and the doers. They are made to envision a future and lovingly lead their families and their societies toward a clear and godly goal. Women are more the nurturers, the relationship guardians, the systems specialists, and the moral guides. Men envision, define, protect, advance, and build.

If you scan Scripture, you find that men are the guardian coaches. They "coach" their children and wives into an envisioned future. They use words to paint pictures of possibilities on the heart. They make the home and the nation safe, they make sure the details don't define the vision, and they exhibit a kind of holy dissatisfaction, which is what moves them to take hold of a better world.

God made man to be somebody—not just to have things

BROTHERHOOD JOURNAL

dness grace mercy love faith goodness truth freedom hope
orgiveness peace humble holiness obey repent perfect submit
serve fellowship comforter transformed noble character church

Society needs men in their fully redeemed form to build godly children, build impacting churches, and build a righteous nation. The reason Christians find true manhood in such short supply in their churches is that they tend to emphasize one part of the gospel. It is true that the gospel is about relationships, morals, family, and order. These are needed, but these are the feminine side. The other side is important as well: the vision, dominion, confrontation, and building side. The two sides together produce a church people want to join and change the world with. One side to the exclusion of the other means imbalance, stagnation, and boredom.

So says the LORD, Cursed is the man who trusts in man.
Jeremiah 17:5 MKJV

Manhood is a powerful force, one that makes a family whole, a woman safe, a child confident, and a community strong. It must be grown, guarded, and transmitted from generation to generation. Without the genuine version of manhood, women become bitter, children become rebellious, and a society often degenerates into the sensual and the small. True manhood calls a people to be better, to seek more, and to find a rowdy kind of joy in the journey.

words
to live by

Things you might not know about *man:*

❶ Historians have recognized that one sign of a declining society is a crisis in the definition of manhood. In fact, among the historic signs of a civilization in a downward spiral are homosexuality, high divorce rates, and men abandoning their responsibilities.

❶ A recent survey reported that while earlier generations complained of churches filled with women yet with few men, the trend today is in the opposite direction. It is not uncommon now to have churches filled more with men than with women.

When God measures a man, He puts the tape around the heart instead of the head.

INDIANA GAZETTE

The proud man hath no God; the envious man hath no neighbor; the angry man hath not himself. What good then, in being a man, if one has neither himself nor a neighbor nor God?

JOSEPH HALL

God made man upright; but they have sought out many schemes.

Ecclesiastes 7:29 NKJV

God, teach me to encourage godly manhood, honor godly manhood, reward godly manhood, and pass godly manhood to the next generation.
—Amen.

man

less grace mercy love faith goodness truth freedom hope
forgiveness peace humble holiness obey repent perfect submit
serve fellowship comforter transformed noble character church

The Remembrance of the Righteous

words
to live by

me·mo·ri·al, noun.

1. that which preserves remembrance.
2. that which relates to memory.
3. a commemoration of past glory
4. **Biblical:** that which makes one mindful of good.
5. **Personal:** a marker of meaningful milestones in your life.

me·mo·ri·al

The angel answered, "Your prayers and gifts to the poor have come up as a memorial offering before God. Now send men to Joppa to bring back a man named Simon who is called Peter.

Acts 10:4–5 NIV

He was a Gentile but he was a good man. He honored the ethics of the Jews, prayed at the times they prayed, and gave generously to the poor. He was considered a "devout and god-fearing man," the kind of Gentile who loved the Jews and their ways.

Surprisingly, he was also a military man. He commanded some one hundred soldiers as part of the famed "Italian Regiment." He was no pansy, no lightweight. He could not have done his job unless he was tough, competent, and smart.

What is amazing about his story is that God chose him to host one of the most glorious moments in history. God had already poured out his Spirit on the Jews. That happened at the Day of Pentecost when the 120 gathered in the upper room received the gift of God's Spirit. Some call this the birthday of the church. With this done, God began looking for a time and place to pour out his Spirit on the Gentiles. He must have considered a great many people, but one came to his notice.

The man's name was Cornelius. He was at prayer at three in the afternoon, the time the Jews normally prayed, the time of the evening incense. An angel appeared to him as he talked to his God. "Your prayers and gifts to the poor have come up as a memorial offering before God," he said. And he sent the man to find the apostle Peter.

Cornelius could not have understood what was about to happen. God was about to unleash the Gentile Pentecost, an outpouring of the Holy Spirit among non-Jews, right in Cornelius's living room. The Lord had considered other men for this privilege, certainly. But Cornelius's gifts to the poor had reminded God that he was there, or, in the language of the angel, "had come up as a memorial offering" before God.

This is what a memorial is: a reminder, usually a physical object that invokes memory. But this is more than just recall. Righteous remembering is essential to righteous living. Psalm 88:12 asks the question, "Can righteousness be done in a land of forgetfulness?

The answer is no. People need to remember, and, in their remembering they need to remind God of their gratitude for his past goodness, of the sins from which he has delivered them, of their prayers over the years, and of the sacrifices of their fathers.

> It is a curse for a man's memory to be wiped from the face of the earth. Let us be remembered in the memorials of the next generation.
>
> HAROLD PAUL

ness grace mercy love faith goodness truth freedom hope
orgiveness peace humble holiness obey repent perfect submit
erve fellowship comforter transformed noble character church

The Remembrance of the Righteous

And they are a more righteous people for their remembering.

The patriarchs of the Old Testament left monuments wherever they went. Sometimes it was just a few stones stacked one upon the other. Sometimes the stones meant so much that they named them, as when Samuel called one stone Ebenezer, meaning "stone of help," and said, "Thus far has the Lord helped us." At other times, the patriarchs built altars, to remember their most meaningful moments with God.

Memorials help believers hold on to the memories that should define a righteous life. They are how the faithful honor their experience and ask God to take note of it.

Aaron shall bear their names [of the tribes] before the LORD on his two shoulders for a memorial.

Exodus 28:12 NASB

Take a moment to identify the memorials in your life. Perhaps you'll think of personal or family rituals that embed faith and memory more deeply than before. Perhaps you'll think of an object that prompts memories. Or perhaps you'll build a memorial in the heart of God through your giving and your prayers. It is by such memorials that you commemorate the good, remind God and yourself of your hopes, and extend the noble into your future.

words
to live by

Things you might not know about *memorial:*

① Sociologists say that memorials begin to appear in the development of a culture once that culture becomes concerned about future generations.

① Personal memorials are a way of honoring experience, of remembering the past, and of carrying its lessons into a more fruitful future.

All these were honored in their generations, and were the glory of their times. There be of them, that have left a name behind them, that their praises might be reported. And some there be, which have no memorial: who are perished, as though they had never been; and are become as though they had never been born; and their children after them.

THE APOCRYPHA

Our lives should leave behind both altars and wells: memorials to the grace of God.

FUCHSIA PICKETT

Your name, O LORD, is everlasting, Your remembrance, O LORD, throughout all generations.

Psalm 135:13 NASB

God, remember me and remember my prayers before you. Help me to remember, as well, all of your goodness to me, the faith of the believers who have gone before, and the words you have given me to live my life by. Remember me, God, as I remember you and your ways.
—Amen.

m · e · m · o · r · i · a · l

na·tion, noun.

1. a politically organized nationality.
2. a territorial division containing a body of people.
3. a tribe or federation of tribes.
4. *Biblical:* a people identified by a common characteristic.
5. *Personal:* the tribe or people group you belong to.

na·tion

Jesus came and spoke to them, saying, All authority is given to Me in Heaven and in earth. Therefore go and teach all nations, baptizing them in the name of the Father and of the Son and of the Holy Spirit.

Matthew 28:18–19
MKJV

It was an amazing moment. Jesus had been raised from the dead just a month and a half before. Since then, he had made appearances from time to time: to the disciples, to the two on the road to Emmaus, to several groups of women. Then the time had come for him to ascend to heaven. He was standing on a mountaintop with his disciples. As together they looked out for miles in every direction, Jesus told his disciples that he had won all authority in heaven and in earth back from the devil. Then came the words that would define the mission of his followers for generations to come: "Go . . . teach all nations."

The words are so important that you should try to understand them in the original language. First, the word *teach* is not the best translation here. The Greek word is *mathetes*, normally the word that is translated "disciple." And the word *nation* certainly has to be better understood. It

words
to live by

does not mean just political nation, as in Germany or Uganda. It means "people identified by any common characteristic." It can mean all schoolteachers, all black people, all Mexicans. It means any tribe or group of people who have something in common.

Understanding this language frees the meaning. Jesus did not look at his disciples and say, "You are Jews. Go to nationalities other than your own and preach the gospel." Instead, he said, "Go to all the different tribes of the earth—all the different groups that orient around certain characteristics or certain experiences—apply the gospel in a way they can understand it, and make them followers of Jesus so they fulfill their purpose to the glory of God."

This is a liberating understanding. Usually, people think of the Great Commission as an evangelistic commission: "Go get people saved." This is part of the picture, but it is narrow and doesn't recognize what Jesus was saying about how people define themselves. Jesus was saying something broader: "Look, guys: there are people out there in the world who are doing all kinds of things and whose lives are shaped by all kinds of issues and experiences. I care about those things. So go make my message relevant to them. Then they can follow me and fulfill my design for them."

How wonderful to think of the nations not just as political entities but as all the diverse races, professions, cultures, and styles of humankind. Understanding that

> We have preached the gospel to reach the human heart. Now we must preach the gospel to reach the nations dear to God's heart.
>
> **DOUGLAS LAYTON**

ness grace mercy love faith goodness truth freedom hope
rgiveness peace humble holiness obey repent perfect submit
rve fellowship comforter transformed noble character church

The Tribes of Human Diversity

Jesus wanted his people to reach them using the "handle" of who they are means several things. First, it won't just be professional missionaries who reach some of the nations. It will be people who are part of them. Who better to reach a biker than a biker? Second, a black person doesn't stop being black when he or she becomes a believer. He becomes a better black person because he begins to fulfill his purpose. He follows Jesus into the reason Jesus made him who he is. Finally, what a wonderfully exciting place the church can be if this is the kind of Great Commission that produces it! All those styles and experiences and ways of doing things, all captured for Jesus and made truly alive by his Spirit. Built this way, the Church would be the most beautiful and exciting place on earth!

The LORD destroys the plans and spoils the schemes of the nations. But what the LORD has planned will stand forever. His thoughts never change.

Psalm 33:10–11 CEV

What "nation" are you part of? You definitely have a nation in the sense that you are part of certain tribes. Have you thought about what they might look like if they were fully captured for Jesus? And how you are called to go into your tribes and make them followers of your King? Such a time as this may be one of the very reasons you have "come to the kingdom."

words
to live by

Things you might not know about *nation:*

❶ Those who live in the West are used to Christianity prevailing in their culture. But this isn't true for most of the world. There are more than eleven thousand people groups in the world that are unreached by the Christian message.

❶ It seems that people need to see the application of the gospel to their "tribe" before they will accept it for themselves. Among the greatest reasons for people of a given culture rejecting the gospel is that they do not see the relevance of the gospel to that culture.

na·tion

Nations are simply people gathered by common experience.
CHRISTOPHER SYNN

Nations are more than political. They are cultural, sentimental, and filial. As soon as the Church understands this we may indeed see the nations offering glory to God.
ADNAN MALOTTKI

My house shall be called a house of prayer for all nations.
Isaiah 56:7 NKJV

God, show me the tribes I belong to in a fresh light and let me reach them with your love, free them with your power, and train them to fulfill their destiny in you.
—Amen.

uness grace mercy love faith goodness truth freedom hope
orgiveness peace humble holiness obey repent perfect submit
serve fellowship comforter transformed noble character church

no·ble, adjective.

1. possessing outstanding qualities.
2. having superiority of mind, character, ideals, or morals.
3. of high birth or exalted rank.
4. *Biblical:* being kingly, having traits or authority worthy of a king.
5. *Personal:* having the inner virtues that move you to Christlikeness.

no·ble

The word noble in Greek is *eugenes*. It means "well-born" or "as being from a good family" or "race." The problem is, most people aren't well-born or from a good family. Even if they are, not every part of their life will reflect their nobility.

But the gospel is about changing all of that. You soon learn after you come to Jesus that you can be well-born by faith and have the characteristics of such nobility by the work of the Spirit.

Consider the story of Jabez. In 1 Chronicles 4, his story is told in one paragraph. He had one of those mothers, you see. She had experienced pain in giving Jabez birth, so she named him according to her experience: *Jabez* means "pain." Think of it. On the playground, when he was called to dinner, or when he was tucked into bed, his name reinforced the truth that he came into the world causing

> Those who are noble plan noble things, and by noble things they stand.
> **Isaiah 32:8** NRSV

words
to live by

his mother pain. He reminded her of her difficulty every time she looked at him. And what else might he have endured from her. She was, after all, the kind of woman who would warp a child's life around her own past pain. It could not have been a healthy environment for the boy.

But now you have to use your sanctified imagination. For if you look carefully, you find that the story of Jabez is only mentioned as part of the chronology of Judah. You should remember that Judah had been given words to define her destiny and all who are part of Judah were part of that heritage by faith. You can imagine that around the fire at night, the tribal elders told of the day that Jacob blessed his sons and said of Judah that the scepter would be his and that the obedience of the nations would belong to him as well. He would be like a lion. How these words must have thrilled young Jabez, for he was hearing who he was as part of his tribe.

Over the years he would hear the story of his tribe again and again, each time the words forming a more powerful force in his soul. Soon the inner image of his destiny came in conflict with the life he was living as defined by his mother's pain, and he could stand it no longer.

"Oh that you would bless me," he cried out to God, "and enlarge my territory! Let your hand be with me, and keep me from harm so that I will be free from pain!"

If one but tell a thing well, it moves on with undying voice, and over the fruitful earth and across the sea goes the bright gleam of noble deeds ever unquenchable.

PINDAR

151

unless grace mercy love faith goodness truth freedom hope
orgiveness peace humble holiness obey repent perfect submit
erve fellowship comforter transformed noble character church

Refusing to Live Small

It was the kind of prayer that changes a life forever. Jabez asked God to remove the curse, protect him, and let his life be defined by the blessing of God rather than the cursing of those around him. "Let past pain no longer shape my future," he prayed. "Instead, let the blessing define me, now and forever."

It is a beautiful story. Yet the entire paragraph that tells it begins with this sentence: "Jabez was more honorable than his brothers." It was what the Bible calls honor that drove Jabez to rise above his past, rise above even the deformities of his mother's soul, and live the large and bountiful life God had ordained.

In a large house there are utensils not only of gold and silver but also of wood and clay, some for special use, some for ordinary.

2 Timothy 2:20 NRSV

This, then, is the nobility to which you are all called in Jesus. To break the curse, to live character beyond your station, to refuse to let biology be destiny: This is the power of your re-definition in Christ. You walk in it by saying, "No more. I want the best God has for me. O God, hear my cry." It is then that the adventure begins.

words
to live by

Things you might not know about *noble*:

1 In history, the word *noble* was used to describe a station or position until the characteristics of nobility were found more among people of low station. Men then used the word to describe good qualities and character.

1 In literature, the word *noble* is often used in connection with the word *bearing*, meaning how one carries himself. The assumption is that one's character is portrayed in one's style or outer life.

Be good, sweet maid, and let who will be clever;
Do noble things, not dream them, all day long;
And so make life, and death, and that for ever
One grand sweet song.
CHARLES KINGSLEY

Political society exists for the sake of noble actions, and not of mere companionship.
ARISTOTLE

My heart is stirred by a noble theme as I recite my verses for the king.
Psalm 45:1 NIV

God, I yearn to live beyond the pain of my past, the curses of those who have wounded me, and the definition of those who have not understood what I am made to be. O that you would bless me, enlarge my life, protect me, and grant me to live free of pain.
—Amen.

n · o · b · l · e

ndness grace mercy love faith goodness truth freedom hope
orgiveness peace humble holiness obey repent perfect submit
erve fellowship comforter transformed noble character church

The Liberating Voice of Authority

o·be·di·ence, noun.

1. acquiescence to a command.
2. an act in submission to authority.
3. fulfillment of an expectation.
4. **Biblical:** compliance with the voice of authority.
5. **Personal:** a lifestyle of deference to God's will.

o · be · di · ence

The call to obedience is disturbing, isn't it? Human beings are naturally oriented toward freedom, choice, and doing what feels good. Any insistence on obedience is jarring to the soul. This is particularly true in Western nations where democracy and individual liberties have taken on near-religious status.

We ought to obey God rather than men.
Acts 5:29 KJV

Christians can love the Western tradition of freedom and individual rights, but they must see the matter of obedience in a biblical light. The Scriptures say that humans can't do whatever feels good to them because sin has damaged their "feeler." Their hearts, the part of them that indicates what is right and wrong, has been damaged and can't be relied on for accurate information. In fact, the Bible says that the heart is deceitful, is wicked, and cannot be trusted. To put it another way, the inner instrument panel of a human doesn't give accurate information about how to fly.

words
to live by

This leads to the matter of obedience. Obedience means relying on an authority outside of yourself to know how to fly, to know how to live your lives. You can't trust yourself, so you have to rely upon God, his Word, and the leaders he puts in your life.

The word *obedience* literally means, "to hear under authority." The focus is on allowing a voice other than your own to shape your thinking and actions. You comply with that voice because you know that it comes from God and is consistent with the truths of Scripture. Obedience, then, is the practical step you take to fulfill the counsel of godly authority in your life.

You have to be honest: This is scary. Immediately, images of robotic religious cults spring to mind. You may start to feel the fear of losing control, the uncertainty of living in terms of outside authority. You may want to retreat into the familiar, self-defined life you've been living.

Yet the question still is, "How has this worked out? Are you really living the life you were made for by living under your own authority and counsel? Do you really see yourself and the truth clearly enough to be your own guide?"

The answer to these last questions is, certainly, no. This is why God tells his leaders that he gives them authority to "build us up, not to tear us down." Believers need coaching. They need objectivity. They need someone they are willing to hear on the issues of their lives.

We are born subjects, and to obey God is perfect liberty. He that does this shall be free, safe, and happy.
SENECA

You have to face something about yourself, though. Human beings tend toward rebellion. It comes from your first father, Adam, who rebelled against God and planted the seeds of rebellion in the human heart. You have, as a child of Adam, the nature of the nonconformist, a drive toward rejection of authority and definition of your life from without. It is what you have become because of the fall, and unless you lean into the freedom from that rebel nature that salvation offers, you will never be whole, never be fully God's, and never fulfill your destiny. Even Jesus had to obey, and he was perfect. How much more is this true of those children of Adam who are growing into children of God.

> To obey is better than sacrifice.
> I Samuel 15:22 NIV

❶

The question is this: What issues of obedience is God pressing into your life? Where is that rebellious Adamic nature expressing itself, and what is the antidote? Perhaps more to the point, who are the human authorities God has positioned in your life to help you walk in obedience to divine authority? Once answered, these questions point the way to the full work of God in your lives.

words
to live by

Things you might not know about *obedience:*

🔒 It is a commonly accepted truth in organizations as varied as the U.S. Marines and the American corporate culture: Only those who can live under authority can ever be trusted to exercise authority.

🔒 Developmental psychologists contend that resistance to outside authority is a sign of perpetual adolescence, meaning perpetual immaturity. The characteristics of youthful rebellion may have their place in the teen years, but carried into adult-hood they will simply prevent the full flowering of potential.

The Christian man is the freest lord of all and the most obedient servant of all.
MARTIN LUTHER

Wicked men obey from fear, good men, from love.
ARISTOTLE

If you are willing and obedient, you shall eat the good of the land.
Isaiah 1:19 MKJV

God, when I became a Christian I made a life-for-life exchange. I gave you my messed-up life to receive the Christ life. This means a life in obedience to the authority of God and his appointees. Give me a teachable heart, God. Wash out the nature of the rebel and make me the person of obedience you've called me to be. May you be pleased with the obedient sacrifices I offer you.
—Amen.

o · b · e · d · i · e · n · c · e

per·fec·tion, noun.

1. the state of being without fault or defect.
2. a faithful reproduction of the original.
3. correspondence to an ideal standard.
4. **Biblical:** the state of suitability for a determined purpose.
5. **Personal:** the fulfillment of your purpose despite your flaws.

per·fec·tion

You are to be perfect, even as your Father in heaven is perfect.
Matthew 5:48 NLT

It is one of the most astonishing commands in the Bible. Be perfect as God is perfect. What an amazing expectation! How in the world could a human being ever do this? How could a loving God insist that flawed creatures be as perfect as he is?

One can suspect that God meant something different from the modern meaning when he used the word *perfect*. Surely he can't mean flawless. Surely he doesn't mean, "Don't ever do anything wrong." That's just too much. And the suspicion is correct. The biblical word *perfect* does mean something different from the modern word.

Perhaps the best way to explain this different understanding of the word *perfect* is to use the words of the American Founding Fathers. When they wrote the Constitution, they said they were designing a government "in order to form a more perfect union." What strange language. You can't be more perfect than perfect. If their first attempt at government, the one under the Articles of Confederation, was perfect, how could you improve on it?

The fact is, the word *perfect* used in the Bible and by the American Founding Fathers doesn't mean "without flaw"; it means "suited to its purpose." The U.S. Constitution was designed to better fulfill its purpose. That's what the Founders meant by "more perfect." And when God told his people to be perfect as he is, he meant "be fitted for your purpose, to fulfill your ultimate design, as fully as God is."

This meaning is also found in Hebrews 5, which says that Jesus learned obedience by the things that he suffered, and once made perfect he became the source of eternal salvation. Now Jesus was sinless, so the process of making him perfect wasn't about removing flaws from his life. He had no flaws. Instead, the process of perfection was about shaping his life—his character, his understanding, his abilities—so that he could fulfill the purposes of God. He was always sinless and flawless. He became suited to his God-given purpose, though, as he endured the processes of God. This made him perfect in the biblical sense, in the sense that he was prepared to fulfill his destiny.

He that seeks perfection on earth leaves nothing new for the saints to find in heaven; as long as men teach, there will be mistakes in divinity; and as long as they govern, errors in state.
FRANCIS OSBORNE

159

Fashioned for a Purpose

What good news this is! God hasn't commanded you to be without flaw. He has commanded you to be fashioned for your destiny, to be fitted for the purposes for which you've been made. It is a call to fit your design, to fulfill the dream of God for your life. Be perfect. Be right for the job. Be what God has made you to be. It is not a command that comes with unbearable pressure. It is a command that means the inspiration to match your highest design.

> God is my strength and power, and He makes my way perfect.
> **2 Samuel 22:33** MKJV

The question now becomes, how do you fulfill this command to be perfect? Like Jesus, you have to allow the hardship and suffering of life to do its work. You have to allow the Father to use even unpleasant experiences to make you what he has designed you to be. And daily you must ask to be put in the school of God's Spirit so that every experience of life is harnessed to make you perfect as your Father in Heaven is perfect.

words
to live by

Things you might not know about *perfection:*

❶ Pastors have reported that some Christians are so preoccupied with their flaws that they never feel qualified to be of impact in the world. This is legalism and a false sense of perfection. The truth is, each life potentially has impact despite its flaws.

❶ The Greek word for perfection, *teleioo,* literally means "to reach its end." The English words *telephone* and *telecommunications* come from this Greek root. It means "geared to a determined end." This is what the Christian idea of perfect is: suited for a determined end.

Perfection consists not in doing extraordinary things, but in doing ordinary things extraordinarily well. Neglect nothing; the most trivial action may be performed to God.
ANGELIQUE ARNAULD

The divine nature is perfection; and to be nearest to the divine nature is to be nearest to perfection.
XENOPHON

I have seen a limit to all perfection; Your commandment is exceedingly broad.
Psalm 119:96 NASB

God, I have allowed my flaws to loom large in my eyes. I have felt disqualified from my calling because I am less than I believe I ought to be. But you are greater than my flaws. I ask you to make me what you have made me to be. Let me be perfect, suited to my purpose, as you are suited to yours.
—Amen.

p e r · f e c · t i o n

ness grace mercy love faith goodness truth freedom hope
orgiveness peace humble holiness obey repent perfect submit
serve fellowship comforter transformed noble character church

pride, noun.

1. inordinate self-esteem.
2. ostentatious display.
3. pleasure in one's accomplishments.
4. **Biblical:** being puffed up with self.
5. **Personal:** the ungodly version of self-confidence.

pride

God opposes the
proud but gives
grace to the humble.
I Peter 5:5 NIV

words
to live by

The Greek word for *pride* means to be "puffed up." In other words, pride makes people think themselves large when there actually isn't anything there. This image evokes the frog that is able to bloat himself to more than twice his size. He looks big, but there isn't anything to his increased size but air. He's puffed up, not truly large and powerful, he just seems to be something.

This is the negative version of pride. It is what results when someone thinks more highly of himself than he ought. He is large is his own eyes, he is confident but only in his own strength, and he thinks himself superior without really having cause. This kind of pride leads to a fall, to sin, and to destruction.

Pride like this moved Lucifer to exalt himself against God and lead a rebellion of the angels. It moved Adam and Eve to aspire to be gods themselves rather than to honor the God who made them. It made

Nimrod build Babel, Pharaoh persecute the Jews of Egypt, and even some of Jesus' disciples dare to ask for a place at his right hand in heaven.

This kind of pride is a lie, a deception. It perverts thinking and becomes a magnet for other problems. Proud people are easily hurt, easily offended, and easily angered. Proud people can't invest themselves in what they are made to be because they are always concerned with how they appear and whether they are honored in the eyes of others.

Perhaps worst of all, false pride keeps people from living in the good kind of pride. The idea that there is a good kind of pride surprises most Christians, but it is quite clear in Scripture. In fact, the New Testament uses the word *pride* in a positive manner more than half a dozen times. God tells believers that they should test their actions so they can take pride in themselves. In the same way, Paul told his listeners they should be proud of him and that his exhortations gave them an opportunity to be proud of themselves.

This kind of pride is what the false kind drives out. The good pride is a kind of confidence, a sense of accomplishment and completion. It is both an attitude and a way of living that draws from a good history in God, from experience that confirms both God's goodness and human integrity. It is what the godly feel when they look at their lives, see the hand of God active in their affairs, and know they are fulfilling the will of God. This kind of pride is what a soldier of

Pride ruined the angels.
RALPH WALDO EMERSON

words grace mercy love faith goodness truth freedom hope
orgiveness peace humble holiness obey repent perfect submit
serve fellowship comforter transformed noble character church

Christ needs to fight the battles of his day, to lead others, and to forge a heroic path into the future.

Righteous pride is confidence in God and his promises. False pride is idolatrous self-reliance. Righteous pride is knowing who you are in God. False pride is assuming a spirituality that isn't really there. Righteous pride is a sense of well-being that comes from godly achievement. False pride draws arrogantly from things, images, and fantasies

> Though the LORD is great, he cares for the humble, but he keeps his distance from the proud.
> **Psalm 138:6 NLT**

Take stock of your own life for a moment. How has false pride puffed you up or distorted your view of yourself? Then again, where have you been resisting a godly form of pride in the assumption that it was unrighteous? Repent of the false, welcome the good, and let the confident humility of righteous pride invade your life.

Things you might not know about *pride:*

1. In classical literature, the word for pride was *hubris*, and it was considered to be at the root of all human ills. In a world where character was believed to be destiny, pride was the most destructive force to human achievement.

1. In Scripture, pride and lies are often connected. Apparently, a man or a woman with a prideful false image will often lie to maintain that image. Lies become the bodyguards of deception.

Pride is the beginning of sin.
THE APOCRYPHA

Pride and grace dwelt never in one place.
JAMES KELLY

A person's pride will bring humiliation, but one who is lowly in spirit will obtain honor.
Proverbs 29:23 NRSV

God, I want to be proud of you, proud of your people, and proud of my history in your ways. I don't want to artificially puff myself up and miss your grace. Help me, God, and give me the right kind of confidence in you.
—Amen.

pride

The Guarantees of God

prom·ise, noun.

1. a statement assuring a future fulfillment.
2. a declaration of intended action.
3. a legally binding guarantee.
4. *Biblical:* God's verbal guarantee to humankind.
5. *Personal:* the assurance you build your life on.

prom·ise

Long before the creation of the world, God was deciding how he was going to relate to humankind. Proverbs 8 hints at this. The Father and the Son were anticipating all that would happen in human history and preparing a way for an errant humankind to return to God.

There is a tendency for people to assume that the way things are is the way they have to be. What people miss when they think like this is the creativity of God. He had options, a wide variety of possible plans for calling humankind back to himself. Of course, they would all have to arrive at the sacrifice of God's Son.

The LORD is faithful to all his promises.
Psalm 145:13 NIV

The system of religion that anticipated Jesus, though, could have taken a different form. Yet God, as the great economist, as the master planner, chose to draw humankind by establishing certain systems of interaction, by causing people to think a certain way and then entering into those ways to reach the human heart.

words
to live by

One of the systems God chose is the way of the promise. The promise is the basis of God's approach to people. It is the promise that is at the basis of covenant. It is the promise that is at the foundation of prophecy, of the possibility of theology, and of any certainty for a religion that survives beyond a single generation.

God established the promise as a method for humans to guarantee their conduct to each other. It came with several assumptions. First, that a promise would be based on the strength of a person's character. Before anyone entered into any agreement with another person, each was urged to consider the quality of the other person. No method of exchange could guarantee success if the character of those who entered into it could not measure up to the demands of the exchange.

The second part of the promise was that words would be considered extensions of character. People were only "as good as their word" because they were their word. Their word acquired validity from their moral nature.

Last in the covenant order was the sanction. "I will do what I say or you can take my children," a man might say. He guaranteed his promise by some horror he would allow to befall him if he broke his promise.

Into this system of doing business came God. He approached people by making promises, and he made promises affirming his character by assuring that no sanction would be necessary. He was as good as his word, and the character that guaranteed his word was

Jesus promised his disciples three things: that they would be completely fearless, absurdly happy, and in constant trouble.
F. R. Maltby

adness grace mercy love faith goodness truth freedom hope
orgiveness peace humble holiness obey repent perfect submit
erve fellowship comforter transformed noble character church

The Guarantees of God

We desire that each one of you show the same diligence to the full assurance of hope until the end, that you do not become sluggish, but imitate those who through faith and patience inherit the promises.

Hebrews 6:11–12 NKJV

the best in existence. So he offered humankind promises so that they would know him and follow his ways. Abraham would have descendents, Moses would lead the people, Joshua would have success, David would rule, Solomon would build, and, if God's people did not stop their errant ways, as the prophets assured, God would fulfill promises of quite a different nature in the life of Israel.

Then Jesus came. He was both promise and the Promiser. He embodied the promises of God, fulfilled them, and then made more. God wanted people to believe his promises, know his character, and walk in his ways. By accepting his promises, humans honored God and received his blessings. This is why the New Testament says that believers have all things that pertain to life and godliness, through his "precious promises."

You must ask yourself: Where have you put your full weight on God's promises? In what area of your life have you put yourself completely in the hands of God's character by taking his promises as more true than your experience? This is faith, this is worship, and this is the human answer to a promise-making God.

words
to live by

Things you might not know about *promise:*

❶ Often biblical truths are confirmed by good scholarship, even when the scholars aren't operating within Christian assumptions. For example, scholars contend that a people are not civilized until they have a mechanism for assuring promises between themselves. In other words, civilization requires covenant.

❶ Human society would fail completely without the power of covenant. All the major human institutions have at their foundation a promise: marriage, government, education, and the military are examples.

Swim through your temptations and troubles. Run to the promises; they are our Lord's branches hanging over the water so that his half-drowned children may take a grip of them. Let go that grip and you sink to the bottom.
SAMUEL RUTHERFORD

God's promises are like the stars; the darker the night the brighter they shine.
DAVID NICHOLAS

As many as are the promises of God, in Him they are yes.
2 Corinthians 1:20
NASB

God, forgive me that I have ignored your precious promises. Let me learn them, believe them, hold them before you in prayer, and walk in new blessing and light.
—Amen.

pro·mise

race, noun.

1. a family, tribe, people, or nation belonging to the same stock.
2. a kind of people unified by community of interests, habits, or characteristics.
3. an actually or potentially interbreeding group within a species.
4. **Biblical:** a people identified by a common characteristic.
5. **Personal:** the broad people group into which you are born.

race

[God] made the world and everything in it. . . . [God] made all nations who live on earth.

Acts 17:24, 26 NRSV

It is one of the most misunderstood scenes in the life of Jesus. He had come to Jerusalem and entered the temple courts. His was enraged by what he saw there. People were carrying merchandise through the courts, and they'd set up tables for selling the sacrificial animals and for changing money into the temple currency. Inflamed with righteous passion, Jesus began turning over the tables and driving out the moneychangers with a whip.

What had upset him so? Was it that business was being conducted in a holy place? Was Jesus simply opposed to capitalism, as some have alleged? Was he making a point about repentance and the human heart?

Perhaps all these are true, but what is often missed is the Scripture Jesus quoted and what it brings to mind from the Old

words
to live by

Testament. As Jesus overturned the moneychangers' tables, he quoted from Isaiah 56. This is not a passage against making a profit or the evils of money. It is a passage that promised the Gentiles they will always have a place to pray in God's house.

Jesus was not upset that business was being conducted near the temple. The fact is, the Old Testament allowed one who had traveled a great distance to purchase the animals they needed for sacrifice once they arrived at the Temple. They weren't required to transport the sacrificial animals over the miles of their journey. They could simply carry money with them and buy the needed animals once they arrived. In other words, the trade in animals and the moneychanging that Jesus saw in the temple was permitted by God.

What Jesus roared against was the racism of the Jews. You see, the moneychangers and the animal sellers had set up their trade in the only place the Gentiles had to pray. Jesus wasn't upset by the business practices he saw. He was upset by the callous disregard for the place of the Gentiles before God. That is why he quoted Isaiah 56. Look at the context of the words Jesus quoted. Isaiah 56 is a guarantee that the foreigners from Israel will still have a place in the temple. Jesus was furious that the Jews had forgotten this guarantee and instead had made the Court of the Gentiles a place of business that could easily have been done elsewhere.

> The sin of racial pride still represents the most basic challenge to the American conscience
> ARTHUR SCHLESINGER JR.

171

dness grace mercy love faith goodness truth freedom hope
orgiveness peace humble holiness obey repent perfect submit
serve fellowship comforter transformed noble character church

The Diversity of God

The lesson is this: Jesus hated racism. He knew that God made all human beings and that the differences among them were to be celebrated, not despised. He knew that racism—that is, hating people because of their racial characteristics—was a sin in the face of God and destructive to the very work that Jesus was sent to do.

That's why Jesus built his church on the strength of love between the races and not hatred. That's why Paul said that in the church, "there is no Greek or Jew, circumcised or uncircumcised, barbarian, Scythian, slave or free." All were to be one. And look at the kind of church this Christian racial unity produced. In the church at Antioch, the leaders were black Africans, white Africans, Greeks, Jews, and a man from what is now Turkey.

> You are worthy to receive the scroll and open its seals, because you were killed. And with your own blood you bought for God people from every tribe, language, nation, and race.
> **Revelation 5:9** CEV

❶

Perhaps you should scan your heart like Jesus scanned the temple courts and look for any vestige of racial hatred. Is there some group you despise or any dark corner where hatred lurks? Perhaps when you clear the temple of your heart, you can take the first critical steps toward a new unity in the body of Christ.

words
to live by

Things you might not know about *race:*

① While it is true that religious leaders in America have often led the way to racial unity and civil right, statistics show that the most racially segregated time in America is Sunday morning.

① Though there have been many hindrances to the preaching of the gospel worldwide, history shows that the spread of the gospel cross-culturally has been hampered more by racism than by any other natural force.

Even though human beings differ from one another by virtue of their ethnic peculiarities, they all possess certain common elements and are inclined by nature to meet each other in the world of spiritual values.
POPE JOHN XXIII

After all there is but one race—humanity.
GEORGE MOORE

I saw another angel. This one was flying across the sky and had the eternal good news to announce to the people of every race, tribe, language, and nation on earth.
Revelation 14:6 CEV

God, grant me your love for people of a race different from me and help me to help your Church become the beacon of racial unity you have called it to be.
—Amen.

173

re·pent, verb.

1. to turn from sin.
2. to change one's mind.
3. to feel regret or contrition.
4. ***Biblical:*** to change one's mind in order to produce a change of life.
5. ***Personal:*** to correct your course in the journey of faith.

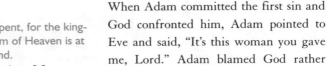

The Change That Leads to Life

Repent, for the kingdom of Heaven is at hand.
Matthew 3:2 MKJV

It is hard for people to admit that they are wrong. They strain to be right from somewhere deep inside, and even when they know they are wrong they strain even to be right in their wrongness. The human family gets this from Adam. When Adam committed the first sin and God confronted him, Adam pointed to Eve and said, "It's this woman you gave me, Lord." Adam blamed God rather than admit how wrong he was. This is the human condition.

Sin has put people in a double whammy. Because they are sinners they are often wrong, but because they are sinners the last thing they want to do is admit it. So they go on covering their wrongness with window dressing designed to make them look right. The problem is that the Bible says, "He who covers his sins will not prosper."

words
to live by

So what do you do? You repent. The Greek word for repent is *metanoia*. It means "to change the mind so as to change the life." You repent when you genuinely believe that you have been wrong and that God is right about the matter. You change your thinking so as to live differently. Repenting is turning. Repenting is change. Repenting is living differently.

But repenting is not just feeling. Paul made this clear when he wrote in 2 Corinthians 7 that a difference exists between worldly sorrow and godly sorrow over sins. Worldly sorrow is just feeling bad. Worldly sorrow is a bad country music song that people sing about things they don't plan to change. You know: "I hurt you, I'm sorry, but tomorrow I'll do it again." Worldly sorrow is the blues people sing because they aren't what they know they should be. But worldly sorrow only gives momentary relief: You cry, you apologize, and you live to sin another day. Change doesn't come because the soul hasn't been touched with the sense of sin's devastating power.

Godly sorrow is the deep understanding that your sins damage people but also, more important, that they offend God. Godly sorrow is the weight of your sins coming to bear upon you and moving you to change. This new understanding that brings change is what the Bible calls repenting, and it is only possible when people move beyond mere emotion to a deep-seated understanding of the tragic nature of sin.

> The best repentance is to get up and act for righteousness, and forget that you ever had relations with sin.
> **WILLIAM JAMES**

unless grace mercy love faith goodness truth freedom hope
orgiveness peace humble holiness obey repent perfect submit
serve fellowship comforter transformed noble character church

The Change That Leads to Life

In fact, you really can't use the word *repent* in the biblical sense and apply it only to the experience of recognizing a wrong. The word doesn't just pertain to seeing what is wrong. It pertains to the change. You can't say "Joe has repented" if what Joe has done is cry at the front of the church after the service. You can only say Joe has repented when months later you see a changed life. This is why Matthew 3:8 says to "produce fruit in keeping with repentance" (NKJV).

> There is joy in the presence of God's angels when even one sinner repents.
> **Luke 15:10** NLT

You have to ask yourself what it may be that God is calling you to turn from in your life. In fact, you may have to ask yourself what you have been feeling bad about but refusing to change. Ask God for godly sorrow—true repentance—and let the course correction begin. There truly is a higher life on the other side of repentance.

words
to live by

Things you might not know about *repentance:*

❶ Christians often fear repentance out of concern that it is a commentary on how righteous they are. But a great saint once said, "There is no holiness without repentance, for we begin in sin and move to holiness by repentance alone."

❷ A famous behaviorist likes to say that the decision to improve oneself on the part of a nonreligious person is the same as the willingness to repent on the part of a religious person.

Repentance is not only grief on account of this or that particular act; it is a deep-seated sorrow on account of the discrepancy between the outward acts of the will and that ideal which is presented to the conscience in the new Adam—the typical—the Christian man.
HANS L. MARTENSEN

Godly sorrow brings repentance that leads to salvation and leaves no regret, but worldly sorrow brings death.
2 Corinthians 7:10 NIV

When the soul has laid down its faults at the feet of God, it feels as though it has wings.
EUGENIE DE GUERIN

God, forgive me for being stiff and unyielding in your hands. I choose to change where my life needs it and to allow the Spirit to bring a course correction to my life. Grant me the spirit of repentance, fruit that lasts, and a life that fulfills your purpose.
—Amen.

re·pent

re·sto·ra·tion, noun.

1. a bringing back to a former position or condition.
2. the reconstruction of the original form.
3. the return to an unimpaired or improved condition.
4. **Biblical:** reclamation of what evil has taken or destroyed.
5. **Personal:** your return to your destined condition.

re · sto · ra · tion

Repent, then, and turn to God, so that your sins may be wiped out, that times of refreshing may come from the Lord.
Acts 3:19 NIV

Jesus said that the devil came into your life to "kill, steal, and destroy." He went to work early. He didn't wait until you were old enough to understand what he was doing. He doesn't play fair. From the very beginning of your life, he used the words of people close to you, wounding experiences, and even your own natural doubts and fears. But his goal was always the same: destroy who you are, take what you are rightly due, and, ultimately, kill you.

Before you knew who Jesus is, you took this condition as normal. You were like the famous story of the man with the ticket to cross the ocean on a huge ship. He was excited about the voyage, so he packed some food, boarded the ship, and thrilled to all the sights and sounds. Every day he would look into the dining area and see the beautifully dressed people eating huge amounts of magnificent food. Then he would return to his cabin and eat

words
to live by

the small amounts of food he brought with him. On the last day of the voyage, a crew member noticed him looking into the dining room and asked him what he was doing. After the man explained, the crew member said, "But, sir, your ticket entitles you to eat anywhere on board. That food you see is for you."

This was your life before you knew Jesus. You were entitled to more, but you did not know it. A banquet had been set for you, but you didn't know you had been invited. Then Jesus comes. He comes having died with your sin, having stripped the devil of his power, and having answered every accusation against you.

And you are saved. You are new. You live in a new kingdom. Then it is time for the restoration of what has been lost. It is a new day.

In Acts 3, you are told that if you repent, "times of refreshing may come from the Lord." It is a sweet thought, but the language doesn't quite convey the original meaning. The words in the original language actually mean that if you repent, the restoration of what has been stolen from you will begin. In other words, it is the sin in your life that has given the devil the opportunity to destroy you. When you repent of the sin, the devil has no place to attack and God begins his restoring work.

Think for a moment of your own life. Think of what has been lost through sin and cursing. From the destruction of your

> Restoration of what our sins have destroyed, of what the devil has taken from us in our days of ignorance: this is the work of Jesus.
> **YUSEF MATTI**

ness grace mercy love faith goodness truth freedom hope
orgiveness peace humble holiness obey repent perfect submit
erve fellowship comforter transformed noble character church

Reclaiming Your Inheritance

property to the damaging of your heart, how has sin made you less than what you were made to be? Think about what has been stolen from you, what valuables have been lost to you, even what you ought to have had from parents, teachers, and friends—all of this is part of what may have been taken from you.

Jesus comes to restore it. He comes, as the Wesley hymn says, to make the blessings flow as far as the curse is found. The very areas of your life in which you have lost the most are the areas he wants to make the realm of greatest restoration and rich provision.

> He shall pray to God, and He will delight in him, He shall see His face with joy, for He restores to man His righteousness
> **Job 33:26** NKJV

Take stock of your losses. Go ahead. Be brutally honest. What has been taken from you? Now, repent of any sin connected to those very areas. And ask God to restore you, gloriously, from his very presence. This is the promise of the gospel and the delight of your heavenly father.

words
to live by

Things you might not know about *restoration*:

1 Under biblical law, restoration was a legal concept that required someone who had stolen to restore many times more than what he had taken. This is the concept of restoration that God says results from the repentance of New Testament believers.

2 *Restoration* in the original Greek means, in part, "to relax." The idea is that one can relax because nothing is permanently lost, because what is lost is returned, and because there will always be more than enough provision.

God cared so much about man's renewal that he sent his Son into the world to accomplish this purpose.
W. CURRY MAVIS

He comes to make the blessing flow, far as the curse is found.
CHARLES WESLEY

When the LORD restores His captive people, Jacob will rejoice, Israel will be glad.
Psalm 14:7 NASB

God, I want to glorify you and bring honor to the sacrifice of your Son by taking possession of all you intend to restore to me. Grant me, I pray, an unwillingness to live in less than you have provided and to repent so as to see all that has been stolen in my life restored. Thank you, God.
—Amen.

r · e · s · t · o · r · a · t · i · o · n

.ness grace mercy love faith goodness truth freedom hope
orgiveness peace humble holiness obey repent perfect submit
serve fellowship comforter transformed noble character church

sac·ri·fice, noun.

1. an act of offering to a deity something precious.
2. the killing of a victim on an altar.
3. something given up or lost.
4. **Biblical:** something offered to God.
5. **Personal:** the surrender of your life and possessions to God.

sac·ri·fice

Your Best for God's Best

David had messed up. For reasons that are unclear in the Bible, David had counted the warriors of Israel. It was a move that offended God. In fact, the Bible says Satan inspired David to do it. So the Lord sent a plague on Israel and more than seventy thousand people throughout the land died. Finally, the angel that was spreading the plague stopped, and he did so over the threshing floor of a man named Araunah.

Sacrifice thank offerings to God, fulfill your vows to the Most High.
Psalm 50:14 NIV

Inspired by a prophet, David went to that threshing floor intending to build an altar. When Araunah saw David coming, he met him, bowed down, and offered to give David the threshing floor when he realized what the King had in mind.

David would have none of it. "No," he said, "I insist on paying you for it. I will not offer anything to the Lord my God that costs me nothing." David bought the land, sacrificed to God, and the plague stopped.

words
to live by

David's attitude is the perfect embodiment of the spirit of sacrifice God is looking for. God is being *merciful*, David thought. *Though I have sinned, he has overlooked my wrongs and prevented greater harm from coming to me. Both in thanks and petition, I will make a costly sacrifice to God. This will please the Lord and may move him to bless me and my people even further.*

Sacrifice, the offering of gifts to one greater, is a natural human response. The little boy yearns to give gifts to his mother. He works all day to draw a picture for her, hoping simply to see pleasure on her face. He wants to thank her, show love to her, and bring her joy. This is the basis of sacrifice.

When sacrifice is first mentioned in the Old Testament, it can seem a strange demand. Men were to take their best livestock or produce and destroy them as an offering to God. In fact, a portion of every man's property was "devoted to the Lord," and, if he refused to give that portion in sacrifice, it became a curse to him. So, dutifully, the people of Israel sacrificed whatever God required, from cakes to cattle.

Progressively, God made it clear that the sacrifice of things was not all he was after. He wanted their hearts. This they showed by obedience, by making a "sacrifice of praise," and by seeing themselves as "living sacrifices."

Self-preservation is the first law of nature; self-sacrifice is the highest rule of grace.
AUTHOR UNKNOWN

This call to sacrifice is central to the Christian life. It is how believers show

unless grace mercy love faith g...
rgiveness peace humble holiness obey repent perfect submit
rve fellowship comforter transformed noble character church

God's ownership of their lives and acknowledge their debt to him. Their tithes, their gifts, their giving up of their time and rights—all these things are ways that they acknowledge they belong to God and that they say thank-you to the One who has shown them such mercy.

Never, though, should they think that they are buying God off. He wants them, and their sacrifices are simply ways that God works devotion to himself into their innermost hearts. God is looking for a people who will live for him, who are passionate about him. The gifts believers sacrifice are important, but they aren't the central issue. A heart that yearns for his presence and his ways is what God seeks.

The sacrifices of God are a broken spirit; a broken and contrite heart, O God, you will not despise.

Psalm 51:17 NIV

Think about your attitude toward sacrifice. Like David, do you nurture a passion to offer God only the costly and the valuable in gratitude for his mercy? And do you perceive your sacrifices not only as due offerings to God but also as God's means of drawing your heart? Do you accept that, ultimately, the goal is your entire existence given as a living sacrifice? This is the offering he seeks and the altar on which he is pleased to reveal himself.

Your Best for God's Best

words
to live by

Things you might not know about *sacrifice*:

1 Among military geniuses in history, few rank more highly than Napoleon Bonaparte. He was often mystical in his military theories and once said, "No army achieves its objective except upon the sacrifices of its every member."

1 Charles Finney, the great nineteenth-century revivalist, once said, "Refusal to sacrifice is not greed. It is ignorance. Only an ignorant man would refuse the true riches that sacrifice brings."

Every Christian truth, gracious and comfortable, has a corresponding obligation, searching and sacrificial.
HARRY EMERSON FOSDICK

To love is to know the sacrifices that eternity exacts from life.
JOHN OLIVER HOBBES

Therefore, brethren, by the mercies of God, to present your bodies a living and holy sacrifice, acceptable to God, which is your spiritual service of worship.
Romans 12:1 NASB

God, make my life a sacrifice. Use my offering of money, time, property, and rights to draw my heart to you. I want to know you. I want to please you. I want to be wholly yours.
—Amen.

s a c · r i · f i c e

...dness grace mercy love faith goodness truth freedom hope
rgiveness peace humble holiness obey repent perfect submit
erve fellowship comforter transformed noble character church

The Investment of Destiny

words to live by

---

ser·vant, noun.

1. one who attends another.
2. one who cares for the needs of a superior.
3. one who sacrifices for another to achieve.
4. **Biblical:** one who invests in the destiny of another.
5. **Personal:** what you are when you care for the needs of others.

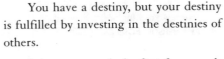

ser·vant

Whoever is the
greatest should
be the servant of
the others.
Matthew 23:11 NIV

Can one sentence change your life? Perhaps, particularly if that sentence captures how you become what God has called you to be and if you own the words in the deepest levels of your soul. Here it is. Please read it and then read it again.

You have a destiny, but your destiny is fulfilled by investing in the destinies of others.

It is not so much the first four words that challenge. Most people know that they are made with a purpose, that God has set a destiny for their lives. This truth rises from virtually every page of Scripture.

It is what follows that should lead to change. Most people who believe they have a divine destiny spend great effort in trying to achieve it. They hear the word *destiny* as if it were the same thing as career or life plan. So they work hard, shine the image, hone the skills, and seek the right positions. They are, in essence, perfecting themselves for the destination of their dreams.

This isn't destiny as the Bible teaches it, though. True destiny is a purpose or a series of purposes God has set that unfold as believers go about their business. People don't create their destiny, nor can they do much to achieve it except to take the next step in God. Always, though, this next step is a step of investment in others. This is because it is only as people invest in the destinies of others that they fulfill their own destinies.

This is the mystery of God's will for your life. In the same way that in losing your life you find it, so it is that, as you leave your life's path to God and give yourself to serving others, you become what you were made to be.

Think of it. A teacher serves others by teaching them what they need to know to rise to their best. That teacher is investing in the destinies of others. But that teacher's destiny is being fulfilled as well. God has designed it this way. So it is with every gift, from pastoring to dentistry, from cooking to book writing.

The model, as in all things, is Jesus. Jesus needed nothing when he was in heaven. Yet when God set a purpose for him that involved coming to earth, Jesus left his riches and made himself a servant to fulfill the will of God the Father. Jesus told his disciples, "I have not come to be served, but to serve." And he did. He taught, he ministered, he healed, he delivered, and he gave

The world cannot always understand one's profession of faith, but it can understand service.
Ian Maclaren

The Investment of Destiny

himself completely on the cross. He spent his whole earthly life investing himself in others so that they could be free and that he could fulfill the purpose of God for their lives. Then, as John 17 says, he was able to say, "I have done the work you sent me to do." Jesus fulfilled his entire purpose by giving himself so others could fulfill their purpose

❶

You have a destiny, but your destiny is fulfilled by investing in the destinies of others. Now ask yourself, where in your life are you striving to accomplish your destiny? Stop. Repent. Ask God to show you the places he wants you to serve others with your gifts. Then rest in him, trusting that his purpose for you will be fulfilled.

words
to live by

Things you might not know about *servant:*

❶ A Japanese industrialist was asked what Americans most needed to know in order to be more successful in business. The man said, "Business is a form of servanthood. Americans must learn to serve."

❶ The great African-American leader Booker T. Washington was once asked how he expected blacks to rise in the troubling decades after the Civil War. "We will teach our people to serve," he said, "and so they will rise as a race."

Doctrine divides but service unites.
NATHAN SODERBLOM

The church is a workshop, not a dormitory; and every Christian man and woman is bound to help in the common cause.
ALEXANDER MACLAREN

Those who have served well gain an excellent standing and great assurance in their faith in Christ Jesus.
1 Timothy 3:13 NIV

God, teach me to serve as Jesus served. Let me leave my future in your hands, take my gifts, and invest them in the well-being of others. Let me do this for your glory alone, God.
—Amen.

s e r · v a n t

---

sin, noun.

1. an offense against religious or moral law.
2. a serious shortcoming.
3. the force of evil in the world.
4. *Biblical:* a transgression of the law of God.
5. *Personal:* a falling short of the will of God.

---

s i n

The wages of sin
is death.
Romans 6:23 MKJV

words
to live by

When God decided to reveal the truths that now are known as the New Testament, he must have given much thought to the language he would use. He had many options, but he needed a language with the right combination of poetry and clarity, of simplicity and depth to allow him to reveal all he had to say.

He settled upon Koine Greek. This was a common language in the Roman world. In fact, the word koine means "common." It was the perfect choice, of course, because it had just the right balance of beauty and scientific clarity to allow full communication of thought.

Yet Koine Greek lacked some words that God was going to need. This would prove no problem, though, because he could always use word pictures. For example, Greek had no word for heaven, so God used the word *sky*. There was no word for offense, so God used a word that refers to part of a trap for animals. And so it went: spiritual truths described in wonderfully poetic ways, making the Bible one of the most beautiful pieces of literature in human history.

God also had to find a word for the concept of sin because Koine Greek had no equivalent. The choice God made is very revealing. He chose the word *hamartia*. It is an archery term, and it means "to fall short of the mark or the bull's-eye." This word picture is incredibly important.

First, God did not choose a word that means "you hit the target but you missed the bull's-eye." This would mean that you have the ability to get close but you didn't shoot perfectly. This makes God a nitpicker: He watches you try but criticizes when you fail. Second, God also did not choose a word that means "you shot way over the target." He did not say, "You're strong but you're wild and I'm not happy about it."

Instead, God chose a word that means "You've fallen short. You try, but you aren't able to shoot to the target. At least, not by yourself. I'm here. I'll forgive you of your failures and help you." What a powerful image and what grace it conveys!

At the same time, this word *hamartia* isn't meant to indicate that sin is a game. Sin is a horribly corrosive, destructive, killing force that people have unleashed in the world through their folly. It isn't just an individual act of failure; it is a spiritual force—what the Bible calls the law of sin and death—that people allowed into the

> He that falls into a sin is a man; that grieves at it, is a saint; that boasteth of it, is a devil.
> THOMAS FULLER

world by trying to be God. Sin is indeed a falling short, in almost every way—a falling short of God, of what it means to be human, of the life that is truly life.

Part of righteousness is cultivating a hatred of sin. This takes some thought. If you think of sin just as something like saying a cuss word or stealing a candy bar, you are close to the truth but haven't let the toxic nature of sin sink into your heart. You have to think of all the suffering in the world to get a sense of the power of sin. Every child who is abused, every life that is destroyed in war, every person who dies a horribly violent death, every family that suffers gut-wrenching trauma—all these are the direct result of sin.

> You may be sure that your sin will find you out.
> **Numbers 32:23** NLT

It is only in understanding the power of sin that you start to understand the grace of God. When Jesus hung on the cross during those six hours, every evil of human existence was placed upon him. Now there is a way out. Sin cannot hold you captive. Repent, turn to righteousness, and find the freedom of canceled sin.

words
to live by

Things you might not know about *sin:*

❶ Every culture in the world, both Christian and non-Christian, has some concept of sin, of wrongdoing. It seems to be a truth embedded on the human soul. In the same way, most cultures have some ritual of redemption, some process by which wrongdoing is cleansed.

❶ Sigmund Freud once admitted that the strongest argument for the existence of God is people's certainty about sin. Freud was an atheist but said he came closest to Christianity when he contemplated its realistic assessment of humankind.

A sinful heart makes feeble hand.
WALTER SCOTT

Sin is a sovereign till sovereign grace dethrones it.
CHARLES HADDON SPURGEON

Woe to those who draw iniquity with cords of vanity, and sin as if with a cart rope.
Isaiah 5:18 NKJV

sin

God, touch my heart with the awfulness of sin that I might also be touched by the magnificence of your defeat of sin in Jesus.
—Amen.

so·ber, adjective.

1. marked by temperance, moderation, or seriousness.
2. sparing in the use of food and drink.
3. sedate or gravely or earnestly thoughtful character or demeanor.
4. **Biblical:** soundness of mind and character.
5. **Personal:** possessing the gravitas that character gives your life.

so · ber

Sometimes the English language falls short. This is particularly true in the English Bible. Entire doctrines can be built on English words that aren't direct translations of the original language.

This is very much the case with the word *sober*. In the common usage, the word usually means "to not be drunk with alcohol." So when the Bible says to "be sober," most people think this has something to do with not drinking too much. Of course, the Bible certainly cautions against drunkenness and the excesses of drink, but this isn't what the word *sober* means in the original language.

The Greek word for *sober* is a compound word that means "saved mind." It means to have the thinking and thus the character of a mind that is consistent with a born-again heart. A saved mind is filled with Scripture, strong against the enemies

Be sober, be vigilant; because your adversary the devil walks about like a roaring lion, seeking whom he may devour.

1 Peter 5:8 NKJV

words
to live by

of the soul, and able to rule over a person's behavior in order to assure righteousness.

When Paul wrote to Timothy that God had not given believers a spirit of fear, but of love, power, and a sound mind, he used the word for "saved mind" at the end of the verse. God didn't want fear to rule over his people, and this is why he gave them a saved mind. The assumption is that a saved mind stands guard against fear and is consistent with love and power. A saved mind is permeated with Scripture and is therefore filled with power that defeats a spirit of fear and with confidence.

This word is critically important because it is intended to challenge the reader. When you give your life to Jesus, when you become born again, you are instantly saved and filled with God, but your soul still needs work. A process of reconstruction still has to happen. Getting saved doesn't automatically change your ways of thinking or the responses of your soul to life's challenges. You still have the imprint of the world's ways and your sinful life on your soul. You need reformatting. This part of salvation is a process, which is why the Bible says that you are saved, you are being saved, and you will ultimately be saved one day. Salvation is both an immediate reality and a progressive project.

Marriage . . . is not by any to be entered into unadvisedly or lightly; but reverently, discreetly, advisedly, soberly, and in the fear of God.
THE BOOK OF
COMMON PRAYER

ness grace mercy love faith goodness truth freedom hope
orgiveness peace humble holiness obey repent perfect submit
serve fellowship comforter transformed noble character church

words to live by

The Power of the Saved Mind

The end of all things is at hand: be ye therefore sober, and watch unto prayer.

I Peter 4:7 KJV

When God tells you to be sober, meaning to have a saved mind, he means you have work to do. You have to renew your mind by the Word of God. You have to memorize Scripture, meditate on Scripture, and apply Scripture to your life. You also have to exercise your senses to righteousness, and this is hard work. In the same way that you gave yourself to sensuality and sin before you were saved, now you have to rework your senses—your loves, words, habits, and feelings—so that they cooperate with the Spirit of God that is in you through the new birth.

①

Consider for a moment what sobriety means for your practical life. Where do you need to rule your passions and acquire a greater self-discipline? What need is there for you to not only reform your way of life but also your way of thinking and feeling about life? Think seriously about these things and ask God to give you the sobriety that makes for an exceptional life.

etcetera . . .

Things you might not know about *sober:*

❶ Many of the ancient writers considered sobriety—meaning the ability to govern one's passions—as the primary characteristic needed by statesmen. In fact, speeches on the virtues of leaders included the word *sober* more than any other.

❶ The phrase "sober as a judge" originally had nothing to do with alcohol. It had to do with the ability of a judge to rule according to the law rather than his own feelings. The idea was that a good judge aligned himself with a standard rather than the whim of his emotions.

No man ever repented that he arose from the table sober, healthful, and with his wits about him.
JEREMY TAYLOR

The sobriety God seeks is not an absence of drink but the mind of Christ ruling man's life.
CHRISTOPHER SYNN

Let us who are of the day be sober, putting on the breastplate of faith and love, and as a helmet the hope of salvation.
I Thessalonians 5:8
NKJV

God, in the true biblical sense of sober, I want to have a "saved mind" that rules over my passions and lets me live the life that pleases you. As I renew my mind and thus my desires, change me and make me a wise and self-disciplined believer.
—Amen.

s o · b e r

197

The Wealth of Nations

splen·dor, noun.

1. brilliant rays.
2. great brightness or luster.
3. a great show of richness and elegance.
4. **Biblical:** the sum glory and majesty of a human or his or her deeds.
5. **Personal:** the glory of your highest life.

splen·dor

[The devil] said to [Jesus,] "I will give you all their authority and splendor, for it has been given to me, and I can give it to anyone I want to."

Luke 4:6 NIV

It would be one in a series of showdowns. The devil would return again and again throughout Jesus' life to tempt him, oppose him, or try to kill him. But this early season of temptation was among the most revealing of all. As Jesus returned from the Jordan River, freshly baptized by John the Baptist, the Spirit of God took him into the wilderness to be tempted by the devil. And the evil one did his best to talk Jesus out of his divine mission.

Among his other tactics, Satan took Jesus to a high place and showed him the nations. The Bible specifically says that "in an instant" the devil showed him all the kingdoms of the world and said, "I will give you all their authority and splendor, for it has been given to me, and I can give it to anyone I want to. So, if you worship me, it will all be yours."

It is interesting that the devil used the word *splendor*. It is a translation of the Greek word *doxa*, which also means

words
to live by

"glory" or "treasure." In this context, it means all the beauty, production, creativity, and wonderful uniqueness of the nations of the earth. It means the songs and poems as much as it means the economics and politics of the nations. It means everything that people do or create with their God-given gifts.

Notice that the devil says he can give these things to Jesus because he had received them himself. The question is, whom did he receive them from? He received them from Adam and Eve. God had told his first humans both to multiply and to have dominion over the earth. Man was to work the earth and care for it. In other words, Adam was to build, grow, create, and achieve to the glory of God.

Yet when Adam and Eve rebelled against God and obeyed the devil, they gave up their God-given authority and surrendered them to the devil. That is why Satan said, when he tempted Jesus, that both the authority and the splendor of the nations belonged to him, because they had been given to him.

That is not the end of the story, though. Jesus did not succumb to the temptation of the devil. Instead, he defeated Satan by dying for the sins of humankind and by stripping Satan of all his authority. That is why when Jesus gave the Great Commission to his disciples, he first said, "All authority in heaven and earth has been given to me."

Splendor is more than a matter of appearance. Splendor is the sum of human achievement, the fullness of talent's gifts, and the richness of man's diversity. Splendor is the glory of man and the honor of God.
Michael Reiveau

dness grace mercy love faith goodness truth freedom hope
rgiveness peace humble holiness obey repent perfect submit
rve fellowship comforter transformed noble character church

The Wealth of Nations

> The LORD highly exalted Solomon in the sight of all Israel and bestowed on him royal splendor such as no king over Israel ever had before.
>
> **I Chronicles 29:25**
> NIV

The story must be seen as a whole. God told Adam and Eve to flourish, create, and build. They surrendered that authority, that power to make splendor, to the devil. Jesus, however, took it back. Then, he sent his disciples—which means you—to reclaim the splendor Adam and Eve lost and to teach the nations how to build, create, and grow to the glory of God.

🔒

What a privilege. You have the honor of restoring by your life and your message the splendor that is rightfully owed to God. Your role in the Great Commission is not just to evangelize, but also to create and build to the glory of God. In fact, this creativity, this restoration of the splendor of humankind, is a form of worship and is how you honor God in the daily work of your hands.

words
to live by

Things you might not know about *splendor:*

❶ The original word for *splendor*, which the Bible says is seen in the nations of people, refers also to the beauty of God. The assumption is that the beauty in the nations is a reflection of the beauty of God.

❶ The word *splendor* comes from an ancient word meaning "a shining ember among the ashes." The idea is beauty among ugliness. This is what God's people are to be in a sin-darkened world.

Glorious the northern lights astream; glorious the song, when God's the theme. . . . Glorious—more glorious is the crown of him that brought salvation down.
CHRISTOPHER SMART

The creation is not utilitarian. God made the earth splendid and the devil has conspired to possess it ever since.
HAROLD PAUL

Consider how the lilies grow. They do not labor or spin. Yet I tell you, not even Solomon in all his splendor was dressed like one of these.
Luke 12:27 NIV

God, I want to honor the sacrifice of Jesus by returning the splendor of the nations to you. Help me to so live and so impact others as to restore what the devil has stolen and to create and build to your glory.
—Amen.

s p l e n · d o r

The Gateway of Destiny

stew·ard·ship, noun.

1. the conducting, supervising, or managing of something.
2. the careful and responsible management of something entrusted to one's care.
3. the improvement of what has been entrusted.
4. **Biblical:** the wise use of God's gifts.
5. **Personal:** the use of your God-given gifts for his glory.

stew·ard·ship

It is amazing how often a single principle of Scripture has the power to save people from a great deal of error. Consider this one. It sounds simple at first, but it is pregnant with truth. Paul wrote in 1 Corinthians 15 that the natural comes first, then the spiritual. Though many applications of this truth are possible, it is tremendously helpful in thinking about stewardship.

It is required in stewards, that a man be found faithful.

1 Corinthians 4:2 KJV

The Greek word for *stewardship* means "one who manages a house," but it is applied in the Bible to the wise administration of everything from food to spiritual gifts. What quickly emerges from a reading of the New Testament is that all believers are given spheres in which they are required to be good stewards. God puts great importance on these areas of stewardship because they are the pathway to the ultimate responsibilities of the Christian life.

words
to live by

In Luke 16, this principle is portrayed very clearly. Jesus said, "Whoever can be trusted with very little can also be trusted with much, and whoever is dishonest with very little will also be dishonest with much. So if you have not been trustworthy in handling worldly wealth, who will trust you with true riches? And if you have not been trustworthy with someone else's property, who will give you property of your own?" (vv. 10–12 NIV).

This is the Magna Carta of Christian stewardship. Jesus' words clearly reveal this principle of first the natural, then the spiritual. Obviously, the question of whether you ever get abundance, spiritual riches, or property of your own is determined by whether you can deal with little worldly wealth or someone else's property. It is your stewardship of the common things that determine whether you are trusted with the uncommon. It is how you handle the daily, the low, and the simple things that determine how you will be entrusted with spiritual gifts and true power.

This is very opposite the thinking common among Christians. Some believers diminish the natural in favor of the spiritual. They accidentally slip into an unbiblical dualism between the earthly and the heavenly. It makes them ignore their bodies, diminish their marriages, undervalue excellence in business, and, often, fail to tend the very matters God uses as a measure of their readiness for more.

As to all that we have and are, we are but stewards of the Most High God— on all our possessions, on our time, and talents and influence, and property, he has written "Occupy for me, and till I shall come."

CHARLES SIMMONS

...ness grace mercy love faith goodness truth freedom hope
giveness peace humble holiness obey repent perfect submit
rve fellowship comforter transformed noble character church

> As every man hath received the gift, even so minister the same one to another, as good stewards of the manifold grace of God.
>
> I Peter 4:10 KJV

The fact is, the natural is the testing ground for your character, and it is character that must be in place before you can bear the weight of the more God wants to give you. Often people pray for more and then ignore the common tasks before them while hoping for better days. God, however, watches to see if they will do common things to his glory. Will they turn that desk or that workbench into an altar and worship God with all their heart? Will they serve others in his name, even in tasks they find unpleasant?

❶

Take a moment to think about the common tasks you find so miserable. Can you rework your perspective in light of Scripture? Can you see these tasks as a test, and as part of an obstacle course designed to prepare you for the greater battles of your life? Once you view your responsibilities in this light, once you become a good steward of everything that has been given to you, you will be on the path to the graduation day God intends for you.

words
to live by

Things you might not know about *stewardship:*

❶ A recent study of great leaders in the last century revealed that the vast majority of these leaders pointed to common tasks they did with exceptional devotion as their stepping-stone to leadership.

❶ The president of a major American corporation recently said that his greatest concern about college students entering the work force is that they exhibited virtually no ability to tend another's property as though it were their own.

Stewardship is what a man does after he says, "I believe."
W. H. GREEVER

Stewardship is the acceptance from God of personal responsibility for all of life and life's affairs.
ROSWELL C. LONG

Let a man so account of us, as of the ministers of Christ, and stewards of the mysteries of God.
I Corinthians 4:1 KJV

God, I recognize that it is the way I deal with the small, the natural, and that which belongs to others that moves you to entrust me with more. Make me faithful, O God, that I might bear the weight of your calling on my life.
—Amen.

s t e w · a r d · s h i p

stir, verb.

1. to cause an especially slight movement or change of position.
2. to disturb the quiet of.
3. to bring into notice or debate.
4. **Biblical:** to impact so as to awaken strong emotion.
5. **Personal:** to awaken the righteous passions within you.

s t i r

I remind you to stir up the gift of God which is in you through the laying on of my hands.

2 Timothy 1:6 NKJV

Part of the art of the Christian life is to know what things you are responsible for and what things God is. It is easy to confuse the two. You wait for God to do what he has left to you or you strike out on your own to accomplish what God alone can do. This means you either live beneath the blessing of God or you live in exhausted frustration. Either way, you don't live in God's best.

The saddest version of this imbalance is to sit idly by, waiting for God to act, when your answer is in your own hands. You grow frustrated. You question your worthiness. Then you question God. Discouragement sets in, and finally despair. But all the while you have what you need if you will only act.

In 2 Timothy 1:6, Paul told believers to take responsibility for the spiritual passion in their lives. He told them to "stir up" the gift of God within them. The word Paul used in the original language is

words
to live by

Awakening the Giant Within

very important. It was a Greek compound word that literally means "up again flame." In other words, when Paul said that Christians should "stir up" the gift of God, he was more accurately saying they should "turn up the flame" of the spirit that is in them.

Notice, though, that he did not say to wait for God to turn up the flame. He did not tell believers to pray for greater flame or call the elders together to intercede for fire. He told them that they had the power to stir the fire of their souls, and that was very good news. In fact, this truth puts the power of personal revival into the hands of every believer.

First, what Paul was telling Christians was something that they should never allow to slip far from their thoughts and experience: They have a deposit of God's Spirit, this "gift of God," within them. They should never take this lightly. In Ephesians 3, Paul told believers that this spirit within them is able to do "immeasurably more than all we ask or imagine." Think of it: Christians have a dynamo from God inside of them that is able to accomplish more than they can even picture in their minds. This means that you have potential in you through God's Spirit that you are actually limiting by your small thinking, small dreaming, and small praying.

Feel the righteous rage.
It is the stirring of God.
Martin Luther

Second, Paul told believers that the spirit in them is like a fire. It must be stirred, stoked, tended, awakened, fed, and allowed to burn in its fullest intensity. This is where passion, power, and the fulfilled potential of God's promises come from.

Third, Paul told Christians that they have the ability to awaken this fiery power from God. By praying, speaking of Scripture, celebrating, hungering, and obeying, believers can stir up the sleeping giant of God's power in them.

I think it is right, as long as I am in this tent, to stir you up by reminding you.
2 Peter 1:13 NKJV

🔑

Try this sometime: Take the portions of the Bible that move you most and read them aloud with passion and zeal. Then pray them to God, including in your prayers that he increase the flame of the Spirit in your life. Notice, as you finish, the almost electrical force that courses through you. You have just stirred the fire of God in your life, awakening the true sleeping giant within.

words
to live by

Things you might not know about *stir:*

1 George Whitefield, surely one of the greatest preachers in Christian history, would regularly go to a private place before he preached in order to "stir the smoldering embers of my holy gift." He was stirring up the gift of God.

1 Martin Luther would often prepare to preach by shouting at the devil as loudly as possible. He told those who heard him that he was "awakening my best heart."

Poor the man who knows not the stirring of his deepest heart.
WILLIAM SHAKESPEARE

Own me. Form me. Stir me. But do not leave me as I was.
MARVIN KINCHASA

While Paul waited for them at Athens, his spirit was stirred in him, when he saw the city wholly given to idolatry.
Acts 17:16 KJV

stir

God, thank you for putting a Spirit in me that is able to do beyond all I can ask or imagine. Teach me to give that Spirit full course in my life, to stir the fire of God in my soul, and to live as the overcomer you have called me to be.
—Amen.

Remembering the Pilgrim You Are

stran·ger, noun.

1. an unfamiliar person.
2. a person not before known, heard, or seen.
3. someone in another country.
4. *Biblical:* a non-friend to whom believers must show hospitality.
5. *Personal:* an unfamiliar person God calls you to assume responsibility for.

stran·ger

I was hungry and you gave me something to eat, I was thirsty and you gave me something to drink, I was a stranger and you invited me in.
Matthew 25:35 NIV

It leaps from almost every page of Scripture: Remember who you are, remember where you have been, and treat others accordingly. It is almost a summation of the gospel. It is certainly how God wants you to deal with strangers.

God calls his people to deal with strangers in light of the fact that they are strangers themselves. The Bible repeatedly tells believers that they are strangers in this life. They don't fit here, don't belong here, and won't remain here. They are pilgrims, people passing by. On earth they are ever abroad, ever away from home. They feel it every day but don't know exactly what it is until they hear the gospel and realize where they really belong. Then they understand and stop expecting to feel in place here. They should ever keep this in mind, particularly when they deal with strangers.

words
to live by

You should try to remember what it was like before you were connected to Jesus. This is part of understanding the stranger also. You were lost, both morally and in the world. Remember that aching sense of rootlessness. Remember the lack of place, of home, of belonging, and of peace you had. You were like Cain, who was made to be a rootless wanderer because of his sin. This is what being a stranger means. It is all the dislocation you have ever felt in a foreign land only more intense. It is hungering to be somewhere you belong and never finding it. This is what it means to be a stranger.

Perhaps because your history as a stranger is something God never wants you to forget, he makes how you treat the strangers you encounter a measure of your devotion to him. This is amazingly the case in the Old Testament. Strangers were allowed to be part of Israel, to worship with Israel, to work in Israel, and to share the blessing of Israel. The people of God were specifically told not to despise, mistreat, or dishonor the strangers in their midst. After all, the Jews themselves had been "strangers in a strange land" and God never wanted them to forget it in their dealings with others.

In the New Testament, the stranger is so important that Jesus even said that to care for a stranger is to care for him. The

> Sometimes give your services for nothing, calling to mind a previous benefaction or present satisfaction. And if there be an opportunity of serving one who is a stranger in financial strains, give full assistance to all such. For where there is love of man, there is also love of the art.
>
> HIPPOCRATES

uness grace mercy love faith goodness truth freedom hope
orgiveness peace humble holiness obey repent perfect submit
serve fellowship comforter transformed noble character church

Remembering the Pilgrim You Are

Do not forget to
entertain strangers,
for by so doing
some people have
entertained angels
without knowing it.
Hebrews 13:2 NIV

stranger may even be an angel, Hebrews says, so you must welcome him or her into your home, feed him, minister to him, give to him of your possessions, and commend him to God. In fact, the New Testament says that you get no reward for being kind to those you know. It is how you treat a stranger that draws God's notice and his blessing.

❶

Now you have to ask yourself this: Have you made it a habit to ignore the needs of strangers? It is easy to do, isn't it? They are the homeless, the migrant workers, the immigrants, those people of odd habits and odd accents. These are the very strangers Jesus has called you to love in his name. This is the mystery: You care for strangers, and yet you are yourself a stranger in a strange land.

words
to live by

etcetera . . .

Things you might not know about *stranger:*

❶ Caring for outsiders has long been a measure of goodness in society. In some cases, this concern for the low had a practical intent. In the ancient world there was a proverb that said "It is the unloved stranger who rises to overthrow the nation."

❶ Politicians often speak of the problem of poverty, but it may be that the Christian church has the answer. It is estimated that if every church in America helped seven poor families prosper, poverty would be wiped out in America.

Much of righteousness is measured by care for the stranger.
WILLIAM RUFF

When one is a stranger to oneself then one is estranged from others too.
ANNE MORROW LINDBERGH

If a stranger dwells with you in your land, you shall not mistreat him.
Leviticus 19:33 NKJV

God, you have said that to love strangers is to love
you. Help me. Cause me to remember that I am a
stranger, that I have been a rootless wanderer, and
that I must help those who feel as I have felt.
—Amen.

s t r a n · g e r

...ness grace mercy love faith goodness truth freedom hope
forgiveness peace humble holiness obey repent perfect submit
serve fellowship comforter transformed noble character church

Cooperating With God's Coaching

sub·mit, verb.

1. to yield to governance or authority.
2. to be subject to a condition, treatment, or operation.
3. to permit oneself to be subjected to something.
4. **Biblical:** to obey the requirements of one greater.
5. **Personal:** to place yourself under the constructive coaching of God's choosing.

s u b · m i t

Submit. The very word invokes negative images. Pictures of slavery enter the mind. People often think of robots, cults and a kind of militaristic conformity. They feel the chill of rigidity and the soul-numbing sense of shutting themselves down to fulfill the demands of others.

> Therefore submit to God. Resist the devil and he will flee from you.
>
> James 4:7 NKJV

Most Christians have had experience with submission, and it has made for unpleasant memories. They may have been in the military and can remember the barking drill sergeant when they hear the word *submission*. Or they may recall with a shudder the domineering teacher who never understood them and never ceased to pile up demands. Perhaps a harsh parent comes to mind, a controlling friend, or the legalism of some organization they once joined. Submission means to them ever ceasing to be who they really are to contort themselves to the demands of others. No wonder they find themselves

words
to live by

wincing when they read the word in the Bible.

The odd thing is, they accept submission as a normal part of life until it comes to submission in spiritual matters. They accept submission to a coach as the price of being on a sports team. They understand submission to airline flight attendants, doctors, tour guides, librarians, and even the teenager who takes their ticket at the movie theater as the price of living in this world. But when told that, to become all they should be in God, they have to submit to believers who intend them only good, they balk.

They don't really understand what submission is. It isn't robotically obeying the every whim of a superior. Submission really is making oneself malleable in the hands of someone who intends good. You cooperate, you yield, you become pliable to the skill, insight, and care of one who will help to fashion you into the best you can be. In essence, you allow yourself to be coached. You don't assume you have all you need to achieve your destiny. You recognize that God has placed guardian coaches in your life. They can only do their work, though, if you cooperate. Another word for *cooperate*, of course, is *submit*.

The other matter people misunderstand is the scope of submission. Nowhere does Scripture require believers to yield their whole existence unreservedly to others. Instead, they yield but with boundaries.

> Submission to God and his agents is the pathway to a docile heart, an ordered life and the fulfillment of destiny.
> HAROLD PAUL

uness grace mercy love faith goodness truth freedom hope
orgiveness peace humble holiness obey repent perfect submit
serve fellowship comforter transformed noble character church

Cooperating With God's Coaching

Wives, submit to
your own hus-
bands, as is fitting
in the Lord.
Colossians 3:18 NKJV

A wife yields to a husband "as is fit in the Lord." A man submits to a pastor only so that the pastor can "build him up." A child submits to a parent so he or she can "grow in the nurture and admonition of the Lord." What these boundaries assure is that one who submits does not become the slave of the one submitted to. Instead, the person who submits becomes the malleable student who is becoming like the teacher.

Take a moment and ask yourself about this matter of submission. Who are the guardian coaches God has placed in your life? Who carries a clear authority and line of wisdom for your betterment? Now, can you gentle your heart before God and become willing to make yourself malleable in the hands he has placed around you? Then do it, and find the solid track to Christian maturity.

words
to live by

etcetera . . .

Things you might not know about *submit:*

1 It is not uncommon for an athlete to reach a high point of success and then become virtually uncoachable. One of the greatest athletes, though, was asked why he had achieved so much. He said, "I never thought I had outgrown the need to be coached."

1 The Greek word for *submit* literally means "to yield under." It is sometimes used of a horse taking the bridle in his mouth. This is very much the image submission ought to prompt in our minds: a powerful being voluntarily yielding to one who knows better.

Submission is the practical fruit of humility.
JIM LAFFOON

Jesus did not submit because he was weak, but because he knew it was the proper response of love and the pathway to power.
JAMES HILARDO

Submit to one another out of reverence for Christ.
Ephesians 5:21 NIV

God, I want to fulfill my destiny, and I believe you have given me guardian coaches to help me do it. Grant me to yield to them—yes, submit to them—as you have ordained.
—Amen.

sub·mit

ness grace mercy love faith goodness truth freedom hope
rgiveness peace humble holiness obey repent perfect submit
erve fellowship comforter transformed noble character church

Fulfilling the Dream of God

suc·cess, noun.

1. a favorable or desired outcome.
2. the attainment of wealth, favor, or eminence.
3. a termination that answers the purpose intended.
4. **Biblical:** an achievement of the good God intended.
5. **Personal:** a life in pursuit of your purpose.

suc·cess

Study this Book of the Law continually. Meditate on it day and night so you may be sure to obey all that is written in it. Only then will you succeed.
Joshua 1:8 NLT

That God wants his people to be successful is without question. He tells them that he will crown their obedience with success, that if they obey his word they will make their way successful, and that righteousness leads to success. Clearly, success is part of the heritage of those who serve the Lord.

The problem, though, is with how people define success. What God has not promised is that he will fulfill any dream of success you might have. This would make him your genie in the bottle obeying your every desire. Besides, some versions of success are quite contrary to God's character. The terrorist's definition of success is that he becomes good at blowing up buildings. The playboy's definition of success is that he gets to be immoral with the woman he desires. The materialist's vision of success is that he acquires more toys. God is not in the business of fulfilling any of these dreams.

words
to live by

So the question is, "What is success?"

It seems that when you take into consideration the whole counsel of God, there really is only one definition of success: God's will. Though God certainly wants to provide for his people materially, give them favor with each other, and keep them from harm, the ultimate definition of success for their lives is that they fulfill his purpose. In other words, to fulfill your destiny is to be a success. This is the key to God's promises of success. He yearns to give believers the grace to become what he has made them to be. Success is the completion of the call, the running of the race, that God has ordained.

This is why God is so harsh in Scripture when he speaks of the false versions of success that humans cling to. A person is never a success because of what he or she owns. Property is a tool, not a purpose. A person is also never a success because of talent. How that talent is used is the defining question. Nor is a person a success because of fame, good looks, or skills. And a person is certainly not a success because he or she possesses spiritual power. In Matthew 7, Jesus said there will be people at the end of time who have cast out demons and done mighty miracles in his name, but he will only say to them, "Depart. I never knew you." Clearly, a powerful ministry isn't necessarily a sign of success as God defines it.

To find his place and fill it is success for a man.
PHILLIPS BROOKS

Fulfilling the Dream of God

In everything he did he had great success, because the LORD was with him.

I Samuel 18:14 NIV

True success is measured in terms of God's will. This is why believers are told that only if they delight themselves in the Lord will he give them the desires of their hearts. In the same way, it is only after they have given themselves to his Word that they can ask what they will and have him give it to them. The reason is, their hearts have to be changed so that they want what God wants. Success becomes possible, then, when they dream the dreams of God and see the same vision that he has for their lives.

🔒

How you define success is among the most important issues of your life. It will determine whether you will be happy in the pursuit. Many gifted people are miserable because they define success quite differently from the success God has designed them for. This is the all-important question: What is the picture of success you carry in your mind? Is it a picture that comes from God? Remember: Success is God's promises. The definition of that success must come from God as well.

words
to live by

Things you might not know about *success:*

❶ Psychologists say that happiness is most often measured by the gap between a person's reality and his or her definition of a successful life. This may account for the great dissatisfaction with modern life: People yearn for more than they can have and grow disillusioned as a result.

❶ A leading theologian suggested that the idea of success in a given culture grows out of the religious values of that culture. In other words, define your religion and you define your view of success.

If you wish to succeed in life, make perseverance your bosom friend, experience your wise counselor, caution your elder brother, and hope your guardian genius.
JOSEPH ADDISON

The secret of success is constancy to purpose.
BENJAMIN DISRAELI

If the ax is dull and its edge unsharpened, more strength is needed but skill will bring success
Ecclesiastes 10:10 NIV

God, make me a success as you define success. Cleanse me of my idolatrous dreams and let me fulfill your dream for my life.
—Amen.

suc·cess

The Heart's Response to Mercy

thank·ful, adjective.

1. grateful.
2. impressed with a sense of kindness received.
3. mindful of past grace.
4. **Biblical:** acknowledging the undeserved favor of God and humankind.
5. **Personal:** your attitude and actions in response to God's goodness.

thank·ful

Enter into his gates with thanksgiving, and into his courts with praise: be thankful unto him, and bless his name.
Psalm 100:4 KJV

A funny but instructive scene takes place in the classic movie *Shenandoah*. In the film, Jimmy Stewart plays the father of a farm family living at the time of the American Civil War. When they pause for prayer before their evening meal, Stewart's crusty character intones, "Lord, we give you thanks for this food. Never mind that we grew it, we harvested it, and we cooked it. We give you thanks for it anyway."

This may bring a smile to your face but only because you have probably felt the same way. You work hard. You enjoy what you earn. Yet you may have a hard time with the idea that you ought to give thanks to God for what you have.

It is this very tendency toward ingratitude in the human heart that moves God to address the issue so often in Scripture. Christians are told that they have nothing

words
to live by

that they have not received. They are warned that it is God who gives them the power to get wealth. They are cautioned that an ungrateful heart is a sign of distance from God and will lead to an immoral downward slide. And they are reminded to do everything they do with a grateful heart, constantly offering thanks to the God who made them.

God cautions believers so thoroughly about gratitude because it is one of the most basic barometers of spiritual health. Believers are rightly aligned with God only when they remember that they are creatures and he is their Creator. This means that what they have has been given to them, even the ability to earn, to create, and to prosper. When people forget God, they begin to think that they prosper and even exist by the work of their own hands. This is foolishness, evidence of a hard heart, and a kind of forgetfulness that leads to destructions.

All throughout church history, Christians have taken care to offer sacrifices of thanks, to pray prayers of gratitude, and to declare days of thanksgiving. They lived in a kind of holy fear that they might forget God's goodness to them and begin to believe that what they had they had earned for themselves. They knew this attitude offended God and moved them out of a channel of blessing and grace. Nothing scared them more, so they made sure that gratitude was kept at the center of their lives.

> Life without thankfulness is devoid of love and passion. Hope without thankfulness is lacking in fine perception. Faith without thankfulness lacks strength and fortitude. Every virtue divorced from thankfulness is maimed and limps along the spiritual road.
> JOHN HENRY JOWETT

...ness grace mercy love...faith goodness truth freedom hope
orgiveness peace humble holiness obey repent perfect submit
serve fellowship comforter transformed noble character church

The Heart's Response to Mercy

Even though they knew God, they did not honor Him as God or give thanks, but they became futile in their speculations, and their foolish heart was darkened.

Romans 1:21 NASB

It was this fear of ingratitude that moved Abraham Lincoln to declare a Day of Thanksgiving around the time of the Civil War. Read his words:

We have been the recipients of the choicest bounties of Heaven. We have been preserved these many years in peace and prosperity. We have grown in numbers, wealth and power as no other nation has ever grown. But we have forgotten God. We have forgotten the gracious Hand which preserved us in peace, and multiplied and enriched and strengthened us; and we have vainly imagined, in the deceitfulness of our hearts, that all these blessings were produced by some superior wisdom and virtue of our own.

Lincoln's words captured both the tenderness of the grateful heart and the holy fear of a leader who saw his people descending into self-reliance and pride.

Your gratitude level is a barometer of your spiritual health, of your sense of reliance on God. Feed thankfulness by rehearsing God's goodness to you and by celebrating even the small mercies of life. You will find that holy passion rides on the wings of thankfulness.

words
to live by

Things you might not know about *thankful*:

1 When George Washington took command of the Continental Armies, he ordered his troops to attend services of thanksgiving to God. He knew that his army would only be as successful as they were thankful to their God.

1 It is intriguing to note that the greatest seasons of expansion for the Christian Church came when its leaders increasingly stressed thankfulness. For example, a maxim of the early church fathers was "Gratitude is the unceasing worship of the humble heart."

Thanksgiving is nothing if not a glad and reverent lifting of the heart to God in honor and praise for His goodness.
JAMES R. MILLER

In thankfulness for present mercies nothing so becomes us as losing sight of past ills.
LEW WALLACE

Let the peace of Christ rule in your hearts, to which indeed you were called in one body; and be thankful.
Colossians 3:15 NASB

God, forgive me that I have relied on self and believed that my own labors have brought me bounty. Lead me in the paths of gratitude and a heart that reflects your mercy.
—Amen.

thank·ful

time, noun.

1. the point or period when something occurs.
2. an opportune or suitable moment.
3. the measurable period during which an action, process, or condition exists.
4. **Biblical:** the realm in which humanity dwells.
5. **Personal:** the measure of the seasons of your life.

time

There is a time for everything, and a season for every activity under heaven.
Ecclesiastes 3:1 NIV

The Stage of Victory

It was a natural thing for them to do. After all, they needed shelter, didn't they? The people of God had been in captivity for seventy years, and now that they were back in the Promised Land, they were understandably eager to build their own homes. Oh, they had done some work on rebuilding the temple, but the work had gotten away from them. Now they had different priorities. The rain was coming, after all, and the cold. They had to get their own paneled houses finished.

Then God sent Haggai. The people of God had not been doing well, and the prophet was going to explain why. It seemed that no matter how much the people had, it was never enough. They had barns full of grain, but it never seemed to meet the need. They had money in the bank, but it ran out before expenses were paid. No matter how much they thought they had, their provision always fell short.

words
to live by

Haggai knew why. The people were not using their time on God's priorities. They worked on their own houses and not his. They were under a curse and, as God said through Haggai, "You expected much, but see, it turned out to be little. What you brought home, I blew away. Why? Because of my house, which remains a ruin while each of you is busy with his own house."

The words stung, and the people repented. They went into the mountains and brought down lumber. They worked hard and finished the temple of the Lord. The result? On the day the temple was dedicated, God said, "From this day on I will bless you." The curse was broken. The people began to prosper, and even what little they had met their needs. They were under the blessing of God, and as the old hymn says, "little is much when God is in it."

In this story is one of the most important principles found in the Bible for the use of time. You do not "save time" by setting your own agenda. Doing your own thing, setting your own priorities, only puts you in a condition of lack, of resources always unsuccessfully chasing need. The most time-efficient path you can choose is the one that reflects God's priorities. Taking care of his will first means that a unique blessing rests on your life so that even what little you have—in time, in money, even in wisdom—will be equal to your need.

You cannot kill time without injuring eternity.
HENRY DAVID THOREAU

The Stage of Victory

Men of Issachar, who understood the times and knew what Israel should do.

**I Chronicles 12:32
NIV**

The Scriptures repeatedly confirm that God offers a peaceful rhythm for life. The believers' times are in God's hands. Believers are instructed to "keep in step with the Spirit," which in the original language means "keep cadence" with God's Spirit. The Spirit sets a pace, a way that Christians can reflect God's priorities and find a peaceful flow to their days.

To find this flow for your life, begin asking God for his priorities for your life and ask him to order your steps. There truly is "a way chosen for us," and the wise seek it out, walk in it, and enjoy both peace and the effectiveness of the blessed.

words
to live by

etcetera . . .

Things you might not know about *time:*

🔲 Asked to list the top three challenges of their lives, a majority of people surveyed listed time management among their greatest needs. Most of these reported that they lacked a sense of priorities that ordered their commitments.

🔲 Human beings are living longer than ever. The fastest growing segment of the population in the Western world is people living past the age of ninety. This fact, and increasing prosperity of the aged, is making the use of time one of the most pressing issues of the age.

Time is our destiny. Time is our hope. Time is our despair. And time is the mirror in which we see eternity.
PAUL TILLICH

To the philosopher, time is one of the fundamental quantities. To the average man, time has something to do with dinner.
J. A. VANHORN

A thousand years in thy sight are but as yesterday when it is past, and as a watch in the night.
Psalm 90:4 KJV

t i m e

> *God, teach me to number my days. Help me to live your priorities, your will for my life. Then I know I will have all I need and please you by how I live.*
> *—Amen.*

Conforming to Destiny

trans·form, noun.

1. to change a thing into a different thing.
2. to change in form, nature, or function.
3. to fit something for a new or different use or function.
4. **Biblical:** to rework a human life into the image of Jesus
5. **Personal:** to be changed according to God's will.

trans·form

Do not be conformed to this world, but be transformed by the renewing of your minds.

Romans 12:2 NRSV

People love stories of lives transformed, don't they? The tale of the homeless man who becomes a millionaire or the child born with a birth defect who becomes a renowned musician thrills this generation. People seem to have a deep need to believe that lives can be radically changed; that the way things begin need not be the way they end.

Jesus came to make just such changes commonplace. Actually, he is an incurable romantic. He believes all people can live their ideal, that no matter how deformed a life might be it can still be made beautiful. And this isn't just what Jesus does in certain extreme circumstances. It is what Jesus yearns to do for all who come to him.

Romans 12:2 grants an insight into just how radically Jesus wants to change your life. Paul said that believers should be transformed. This word is powerful in the original language. It is *metamorphoo* in Greek. It is the word that is translated as

words
to live by

metamorphosis in English, and it describes some of nature's most dramatic alterations. It is, for example, the process by which a slimy caterpillar becomes a beautiful butterfly.

Jesus wants to change you this radically, as much change as makes a caterpillar into a butterfly. Yet Paul made it clear that you have a role to play in this transformation also. He said that you must not be conformed to the world. He used a very powerful word here as well. The word *conformed* is *suschematizo* in Greek. It means "to shape one thing into the image of another." In fact, the word suggests an interesting picture. The last part of the word, *-schematizo*, is the word that modern English renders "schematic." A schematic is the drawing of an electrical system that you get with a new appliance. Putting Paul's meaning in different words, this verse can be stated, "Don't be wired the way the world is wired." Don't have the same response systems, the same values, the same kind of energy in your life that the world does. Don't let the world shape you, but let Jesus transform you into a whole new creature.

Then comes that all-important phrase: "by the renewing of your mind." Paul was saying that you break the molding power of the world and become the glorious creatures you were meant to be if you renew your mind. It means

> When you come to Christ, the Holy Spirit takes up residence in your heart. Something new is added to your life supernaturally. You are transformed by the renewing of your mind. A new power, a new dimension, a new ability to love, a new joy, a new peace—the Holy Spirit comes in and lives the Christian life through you.
> BILLY GRAHAM

Conforming to Destiny

that your problem is your "stinking thinking." Like most people, you sometimes think as the world does, believe the ideas you learned during your days before Jesus, and accept every horrible thing that has ever been said about you.

To use Paul's imagery from Ephesians 5, you need a washing by the water of the Word. If you will read the Scriptures, memorize the Scriptures, meditate on the Scriptures, and actively believe the Scriptures—then the scrub brushes of God's Word begin to wash your mind. To use another picture, the Word of God erases what you've recorded on the tape of your mind and records God's thoughts instead. Then you become as you think, for as Proverbs says, as a man thinks in his heart so is he.

> We, who with unveiled faces all reflect the Lord's glory, are being transformed into his likeness with ever-increasing glory, which comes from the Lord, who is the Spirit.
> **2 Corinthians 3:18**
> NIV

Take a moment to consider this matter of your transformation. God made you to be a glorious being. You are on your way there. The fast track, though, is a renewed mind, a repentant heart, and complete devotion to the Scriptures. Make these a priority in your life and you will find yourself morphing into the Christlike being you are destined to be.

words
to live by

Things you might not know about *transform*:

1 In electronics, a transformer is a device that changes power from one level to another. This is what spiritual transformation is as well: the remaking of one's life to be a conduit of a greater power from God.

1 In classical Greek literature, to be transformed was to experience "the outward expression of an inward state." In fact, hypocrisy was exactly the opposite: the conflict between the inner and the outer. To be transformed is to become what you really are on the inside.

The transformation of personality, through the decisive act of faith, wrought in the individual by the ministry of the Spirit of God, is termed salvation. This moral and spiritual change is also known as the new birth.
ROBERT O. FERM

We were chaff, now we are wheat.
JAMES BISSE

But let me tell you a wonderful secret God has revealed to us. Not all of us will die, but we will all be transformed.
I Corinthians 15:51
NLT

God, transform me. Grant me the power to disconnect from the world, to immerse myself in your Word, and to become the glorious creature you've destined me to become.
—Amen.

trans·form

trib·u·la·tion, noun.

1. distress or suffering.
2. exceptional trouble.
3. severe affliction.
4. **Biblical:** the trouble that befalls believers in a fallen world.
5. **Personal:** the hardships of your life.

trib·u·la·tion

The Greek word for *tribulation* is very revealing. It means "to wear away by the constant application of pressure." It can mean "to grind down," "to defeat by attrition," "to erode by stress." In the Bible, it is translated *persecution, distress, trouble, hardship*, and *affliction*. This tribulation can be low level, but it can also be one of the primary tactics of the devil against the people of God. The book of Daniel says that the evil one intends to "wear down the saints." He does this through the tribulations in your life.

What the devil intends through the tribulations in your life is a number of objectives. He wants, perhaps first of all, to distract you from the next step you are called to take in following Jesus. He also wants to steal God's Word from your heart, as the Parable of the Sower teaches. And he wants to discourage you, to make you believe that God is not for you and that your troubles are a sign of God's neglect.

Our light and momentary troubles are achieving for us an eternal glory.
2 Corinthians 4:17 NIV

words
to live by

The damage that such tribulation does in your life is deepened by your expectations. Modern Christians often accept the lie that life in general and the Christian life in specific is meant to be a rose garden, a trouble-free paradise. Advertising teaches people to expect ease at every moment, and some Christian theology leads people to believe that the truly righteous will never want for anything. It would be nice, but it isn't consistent with experience, it isn't biblical, and it isn't what makes Christians of any strength.

The Bible says that many are the troubles of the righteous, but the Lord delivers his people from them all. This is part of the beauty of the Bible: It is one of the most realistic documents in human history. It does not teach a fantasy religion; it is a reality religion that teaches humankind to storm into hardship armed with faith. The fact is, tribulation is part of life. The issue isn't whether you have trouble, but how you go through trouble and emerge from it that counts.

A more biblical attitude would serve believers well. The Bible warns to expect trouble. Troubles will come, and they will come more for the righteous than for others because the righteous are in a battle between darkness and light. The players on the field always get more knocked around than the spectators in the stands. The Bible also exhorts God's people to prepare for trouble by storing up Scripture in your heart, being prayed up, having a band of brothers against a day of trouble, and keeping a clean life so as not to give the devil an opportunity.

It is a pity that our tears on account of our troubles should so blind our eyes that we should not see our mercies.
JOHN FLAVEL

lness grace mercy love faith goodness truth freedom hope
orgiveness peace humble holiness obey repent perfect submit
serve fellowship comforter transformed noble character church

The Chisel of God

Perhaps most of all, the Bible encourages the understanding that tribulation serves God's purposes. Rightly understood, rightly engaged, and rightly overcome, tribulation can not only change you but position you for the greater life God intends. This was the attitude of Joseph, who told his brothers, "You intended to harm me, but God intended it for good to accomplish what is now being done, the saving of many." Joseph understood that painful though it was, God had used unrighteous treatment, temptations, and the smallness of others to position him for greatness. So it is for you, if you allow tribulation to be a propelling wind rather than a destroying storm.

A righteous man may have many troubles, but the LORD delivers him from them all.
Psalm 34:19 NIV

Nothing distinguishes the spiritually mature like suffering. You can either be crushed by your disappointments and pains or you can see them as the price of the battle and the process of Christlikeness. Take a turn in your heart. Like an experienced seaman, turn your ship into the wind of affliction and ride the storms of life to a better day.

words
to live by

Things you might not know about *tribulation:*

❶ An American statesman once said, "I don't trust anyone who has not known tribulation. It is only after a man has suffered that he is humble enough to trust." That statesman was Abraham Lincoln, who perhaps suffered more in office than any man since who has held the White House.

❷ The word *tribulation* comes from the Latin word *tribulum,* which was the part of a threshing floor that pressed the grain. This is what tribulation comes into our lives to do: press us into usefulness.

If the sun of God's countenance shine upon me, I may well be content to be wet with the rain of affliction.
JOSEPH HALL

The Christian under trouble doesn't break up—he breaks out.
E. STANLEY JONES

We also glory in tribulations, knowing that tribulation produces perseverance; and perseverance, character; and character, hope.
Romans 5:3 – 4 NKJV

God, let tribulation have its perfect work in me that I might be pleasing to you.
—Amen.

trib·u·la·tion

237

wis·dom, noun.

1. the accumulated philosophic or scientific learning.
2. the teachings of ancient wisdom.
3. the ability to discern inner qualities and relationships.
4. *Biblical:* insight into the true nature of things.
5. *Personal:* the perspective of God for living your life.

wis·dom

It was Solomon who, given an opportunity to ask God for anything, asked for wisdom and got everything else his heart desired as well. It was Paul who said that a spirit of wisdom would help believers see Jesus better. And James wrote that wisdom means good deeds and a good life.

Wisdom is the principle thing; therefore get wisdom: and with all thy getting get understanding.
Proverbs 4:7 KJV

So what is this wisdom and why is it so important? The Hebrew word for *wisdom* means "practical principles for living." It seems that wisdom is a way of looking at life that has a practical result. Wisdom is supposed to be the truth or the principle that guides your actions. It is what you believe about a life rightly lived that determines what you do.

The Bible speaks of the "wisdom of this world" that only gets people into trouble. The book of James calls this wisdom "earthly, unspiritual, of the devil." You hear the slogans of such wisdom all the time: "If it feels good, do it" is one such example. Another is "God helps those

words
to live by

who help themselves." Some in this world see these as principles to guide their conduct. For them, these slogans are wisdom. The Christian, of course, feels differently.

For the Christian, wisdom is rooted in the belief that God has set an order to the world, that there is a right and wrong way of doing things. Wisdom is the insight that comes from knowing this. It also comes from understanding that God has something to say about every detail of life. This isn't because he wants to hawk over humankind and judge them for their failures. It is because God originally created people to walk with him in all things. God would have taught Adam about his wife or about business or even about how to conduct himself with his friends. Wisdom would have come from relationship. After the fall, though, wisdom had to come by principle as God drew people back to his original design.

Think for a moment about all the subjects the book of Proverbs addresses. These proverbs are the systematized wisdom that God gave Solomon, and they deal with a huge number of topics: how to behave toward the opposite sex, what to do with one's money, how powerful words are, the damage that gossip does, the value of friends, the misery of a bad marriage, the glory of a good wife, the dangers of the temptress, the way rulers ought to behave, the destruction of haughtiness, the way of the fool, and dozens of other topics.

To have a low opinion of our own merits and to think highly of others is an evidence of wisdom.
THOMAS À KEMPIS

uless grace mercy love faith goodness truth freedom hope
orgiveness peace humble holiness obey repent perfect submit
serve fellowship comforter transformed noble character church

But you should not make the mistake of believing that wisdom is only a list of proverbs. The Bible also speaks of wisdom as a spirit and of the wisdom that comes from having a relationship with Jesus. In other words, wisdom is God's way of doing things, however you come to understand it. It is life-transforming; it distinguishes the wise from the foolish of this world, and it is essential for the person who plans to please God.

Perhaps the best news about wisdom is that God promises it to those who seek it. James wrote that if anyone lacks wisdom, he'll have it if he asks and asks in faith. James is primarily talking about how to get through suffering, but what he says is true for every area of life.

So teach us to number our days, that we may apply our hearts unto wisdom.
Psalm 90:12 KJV

❶

Do you have a tough marriage? Ask for wisdom. Need a change in your business? Ask for wisdom. You aren't seeing the qualities you would like to in your children? Ask for wisdom. Your friendships often go bad? Ask for wisdom. And add to your asking a sincere study of the wisdom in the Bible and you will find the wise path God promises to the faithful.

words
to live by

Things you might not know about *wisdom:*

❶ The usual word for wisdom in Greek is *sophia.* Though used less often, a second word is also very helpful. It is *phronesis.* It means "an ability to discern the results of one's actions in advance."

❶ Many scholars identify the "wisdom literature" of the Bible as the most distinct literary works to come out of the ancient world. Never before in human literature had wisdom been so highly valued and so systematically assembled.

He who provides for this life, but takes not care for eternity, is wise for a moment, but a fool forever.
JOHN TILLOTSON

The good Lord set definite limits on man's wisdom, but set no limits on his stupidity—and that's just not fair!
KONRAD ADENAUER

The wisdom of this world is foolishness with God.
I Corinthians 3:19 KJV

God, make me wise. Grant me to meditate on your Word, seek your face, and never be content until I know your will for every step of my life.
—Amen.

w i s · d o m

love grace mercy love faith goodness truth wisdom hope
rgiveness peace humble holiness obey repent perfect submit
erve fellowship comforter transformed noble character church

Revealing the Nature of God

wom·an, noun.

1. an adult female person.
2. the feminine of the human species.
3. a non-male human.
4. **Biblical:** a female created in the image of God.
5. **Personal:** the female you are, came from, or hope for.

w o m · a n

A woman of noble character.
Ruth 3:11 NIV

words
to live by

A Christian psychologist was asked to explain which aspects of the nature of God are imprinted on the soul of a child by each of his parents. The psychologist explained that a father embeds into the heart of a child God's trustworthiness. It is the father who throws the child into the air and catches him again. Trust is built. It is the father who pushes back the furniture in the living room and wrestles or plays "horse." The result is chaos and noise, but dad can be trusted. Dad is the wild one, the rowdy friend, but dad is strong and safe.

Mothers, the psychologist explained, are the warm center, the safe place; they are "home." They tend to model for a child that God is "there," that he exists and is ever present. It is a mother, after all, that a child runs to when feelings are hurt or the knee is skinned. It is the mother whose presence makes the house a home and makes the home a safe base to launch into life from.

What a mother provides for a child, women provide for society. Though their benefits aren't just domestic, they bring by virtue of their gifts a sense of place, focus, devotion, and emotional energy that not only enriches what they invest in but offers the world the civilizing influence of morality, relationship, and duty.

It is important to remember, though, that largely because of this glorious good that women bring into the world, they are under attack. Satan hates women, as the Bible makes clear, and seeks to destroy them at every turn. Scan the world and witness the catalog of crimes against women. In one country women not properly shawled might have acid thrown in their faces. In another country, women's bodies are legally disfigured at the will of their fathers. In yet another country, women may be killed on order of the men in their families. And in the West, women are belittled by pornography and sexual attitudes that make them little more than toys.

A woman is a glorious creature, a representation of part of God's nature, and the one who most often imparts the sense of greatness to children and to society as a whole. It is a woman who most often keeps the flame of faith burning, a woman who checks the aggressive nature of men and seeks healing for the soul and the nation, and a woman who very often knows how to do what the more visionary man dreams. It is also a woman who has the power to believe in the good of

> The woman was formed out of man—not out of his head to rule over him; not out of his feet to be trod upon by him; but out of his side to be his equal, from beneath his arm to be protected, and from near his heart to be loved.
>
> **MATTHEW HENRY**

one whom others have discarded and a woman who makes sure that the dreamer's rhetoric is played out in the day to day.

You should ask yourself how you are either modeling or encouraging godly womanhood. A man does this by protecting, encouraging, blessing, and celebrating the good that godly womanhood is. A woman does this by guarding against the false versions of womanhood in her culture, seeking to be the kind of woman described in Scripture, and teaming with a godly man to be the full representation of the nature of God to the world. There is a role for every believer to play in this restoration, and few generations have shown such a crying need for it like this one.

Adam said: "This is now bone of my bones and flesh of my flesh; she shall be called Woman, because she was taken out of Man."
Genesis 2:23 NKJV

Godly womanhood is a force to be protected, nurtured, and honored. No matter your gender, you have a role in this. Ask God to give you the grace to fulfill that role and be part of encouraging this vital force in your time.

words
to live by

etcetera . . .

Things you might not know about *woman:*

❶ Aptitude tests reveal that women are superior to men in all areas of aptitude except two: abstract thought and aggression. This certainly explains why a society is much the poorer when women are not allowed to emerge to their potential.

❶ Women are more numerous than men worldwide, live longer lives, tend to be healthier than men, and yet tend to express less satisfaction with their circumstances. This dissatisfaction is normally tied to a personal sense of fulfillment rather than economic or social factors.

Next to God we are indebted to women, first for life itself, and then for making it worth having.
CHRISTIAN NESTELL BOVEE

There is a woman at the beginning of all great things.
ALPHONSE DE LAMARTINE

Charm is deceitful and beauty is vain, but a woman who fears the LORD, she shall be praised
Proverbs 31:30 NASB

God, please restore godly womanhood in this generation.
Let the full revelation of your nature be seen as your
women arise in righteousness in this generation.
—Amen.

w o m · a n

ness grace mercy love faith goodness truth freedom hope
rgiveness peace humble holiness obey repent perfect submit
serve fellowship comforter transformed noble character church

The Perversion of the Mind

words

words *to live by*

wor·ry, noun.

1. mental distress or agitation resulting from concern.
2. anxiety of mind and heart.
3. burdensome thoughts of impeding ill.
4. **Biblical:** fear expressing itself as thought.
5. **Personal:** concentrating your mind on fear rather than faith.

wor·ry

When God created people, he gave them a unique and wonderful mental power. It is called meditation. It is the ability to mentally work and rework a truth, like turning a diamond to see all its facets. It allows ideas to press more deeply into the soul, for reality to take on richness in the understanding that they would never have had without meditation.

In fact, the Greek word for *meditation* is taken from a unique ability of cows. Cows have four stomachs, and they eat, swallow, and then bring up what they have swallowed to chew it again when they choose. This is a good picture for meditation. Human beings hear, think, store, and then bring up what they've heard to ponder it again at will. By doing so, they deepen understanding and allow truth to work its way into their consciousness and thus into the way they live.

It is important for believers to understand what meditation is before they con-

Worry is a heavy burden.
Proverbs 12:25 CEV

sider this matter of worry, and this is for a very good reason: Worry is meditation perverted. Whereas God has designed meditation as a means for Christians to grow, increase in understanding, and live lives of greater depth, worry grows from this same process but is inspired by fear.

Worry is the contemplation of non-realities in the light of fear. By worrying, people take the power of meditation and apply it to possible wrongs, to evils that may happen. They take the power God has given to visualize good and use it to play out scenarios of harm and evil.

The great harm this does is that meditation has a power that is something like planting seeds. Meditation, and therefore worry, expands a subject, grows it in the soul. When people, inspired by fear, worry, they amplify their fears and grow them into strongholds that can rule their lives. In fact, a strong connection exists between fear and worry because the one is the source of the other. Most fears arise because of unrestrained worry. And once this vicious cycle of fear-inspiring-worry and worry-increasing-fear gets started, it moves out to other areas of life like an occupying army. Soon Christians find themselves battling fear and worry in areas of their lives where they had no problem before.

The first step toward overcoming worry is realizing that the activity of worry is replacing the very activity that is the antidote to worry. To defeat worry, which is fear-inspired meditation, believers have to use the power of meditation on good and noble themes to overcome the evil they are pondering.

Leave tomorrow's trouble to tomorrow's strength; tomorrow's work to tomorrow's time; tomorrow's trial to tomorrow's grace and tomorrow's God.

AUTHOR UNKNOWN

247

uness grace mercy love faith goodness truth freedom hope
orgiveness peace humble holiness obey repent perfect submit
serve fellowship comforter transformed noble character church

The Perversion of the Mind

You will rest safe
and secure, filled
with hope and
emptied of worry.
Job 11:18 CEV

You can't battle worry by choosing not
to think. You will always think. The task at
hand is to think on different things. In a
sense, you have to overcome evil with good
in your thought life. Where you are anticipating destruction and worrying about it,
you have to think on God's promises of pro-
tection. Where you meditate on some lack
you think might befall you, you have to
consider God's provision in the past and his
promises to sustain you. This is how you do
a kind of spiritual warfare of the mind and
so defeat both fear and worry.

*Take a moment to do an inventory of
your worries. The last time worry kept
you awake at night, what was its theme?
The last time you found your thoughts
running to concerns that robbed you of
joy, what were those thoughts? Make a
list of them, find Scriptures that answer
them, and use the godly power of meditation to overcome the encroachment of
worry.*

words
to live by

etcetera . . .

Things you might not know about *worry*:

❶ A recent medical journal article has identified intense worry as a major threat to good health. It seems that worry takes a specifically physical toll on the human body, weakening it and making it susceptible to disease.

❶ An international corporation named worry as the primary force that leads to mistakes on the job. It appears that worry is such a distraction factor that workers can't concentrate on their work.

Anxiety springs from the desire that things should happen as we wish rather than as God wills.
CHRISTOPHER SYNN

All worry is atheism, because it is a want of trust in God.
BISHOP FULTON J. SHEEN

Do not worry about your life, what you will eat; or about your body, what you will wear. Life is more than food, and the body more than clothes.
Luke 12:22–23 NIV

God, by giving myself to worry I have crowded out your Word and fed fear in my life. Forgive me. Reverse the process and help me to work your words into my life so deeply that I am transformed and worry is banished.
—Amen.

wor·ship, noun.

1. the reverence offered a divine being or supernatural power.
2. a form of religious practice with its creed and ritual.
3. extravagant respect or admiration.
4. **Biblical:** the payment of homage to, the honoring of.
5. **Personal:** the way your life expresses the worth of God.

wor·ship

God is a Spirit: and they that worship him must worship him in spirit and in truth.
John 4:24 KJV

Proverbs 8 seems to tell the story well. The subject, of course, is wisdom, but the sense is that it is Jesus who is actually speaking. He is talking about being there when God made the worlds and gracing the acts of creation.

Then comes a moving phrase. It says that God the Father and this Jesus/Wisdom figure were delighting in each other before the creation of the world. What a picture the words paint. Before anything was created, this God the Father, who is love, was delighting in his Son. The two were lavishing each other with honor and praise, with love and tenderness. It is this passion of the Godhead for each other that becomes the loving basis of all of creation.

It is not hard to imagine that God made people to share in this love, this holy passion. The Father and the Son wanted other creatures to share the delight they felt for each other. So humans were made,

words
to live by

beings capable of knowing and returning the love of God. It was not just that this delighting, this worship, was something people ought to do. People were made for it. It completed who they were because they were made to participate in this love and delight of the Godhead.

People fell into sin, of course, and they fell because they wanted to be like god rather than to worship and delight in the only real God. It is interesting that the being who tempted Eve to believe that she and Adam could be gods knew that humans could never be gods. Satan had been a heavenly creature who grew to covet the heavenly worship offered to the Creator. Cast down from heaven for his rebellion and desire to be god, Satan conspired to draw people after himself. So he told a lie. He told them they could be their own god. But they couldn't. Humans have to serve somebody, have to worship something. So Satan told them they could be their own god when Satan actually knew they would end up under his evil power if they rejected God. Thus, the fall of humanity and the rule of evil in the world.

God had a plan, though, and that plan was as much about restoring humans to rightful worship as it was anything else. God taught his fallen creatures about worship, about sacrifice, and about offerings. When he delivered his captive people from Egypt, it was about worship: "Let my people go that they might worship me," he said. When he established his Jewish Kingdom, he put worship at the center of it. When he temporarily rejected

> They that worship merely from fear, would worship the devil too, if he appear.
> **PROVERB**

ess grace mercy love faith goodness truth freedom hope
rgiveness peace humble holiness obey repent perfect submit
erve fellowship comforter transformed noble character church

his people and sent them into captivity, it was about their insistence on worshiping other gods. Yet when his people worshiped him with pure hearts, the Lord did miracles for them.

Then Jesus came. He told the people that their controversies about methods of worship were silly. He said that God is looking for those who will worship him in spirit and in truth. True worship isn't about utensils and temples, he said. It's about returning to that delighting and tender love that the Father and Jesus had known before time. And worship was restored.

I urge you, brethren, by the mercies of God, to present your bodies a living and holy sacrifice, acceptable to God, which is your spiritual service of worship.
Romans 12:1 NASB

●

Clearly, part of the destiny of every believer is to worship. Worship is the fulfillment of the relationship with the Father that Jesus came to make possible. Consider, for a moment, your worship life. Do you worship? Do you only worship in church or when you are alone? Do you find that God meets you as you lavish honor on him? These are the questions that may well lead you to the life of worship that pleases the heart of God.

words
to live by

Things you might not know about *worship:*

1 A study of various religions in the Third World confirmed that most converts to new religions are first drawn by the beauty of worship. It seems that often the sense of "holiness" about a religion is its greatest draw to the uninitiated.

1 Sociologists tell us that all people groups, even those without a religion of transcendence, practice rituals that are forms of worship. In fact, worship is one of the factors that most defines the various people groups of the earth.

It is only when men begin to worship that they begin to grow.
CALVIN COOLIDGE

Man worships because God lays His hand to the dust of our experience, and man miraculously becomes a living soul—and knows it and wants to worship.
DOUGLAS HORTON

Thou shalt worship no other god: for the LORD, whose name is Jealous, is a jealous God.
Exodus 34:14 KJV

God, you have made me to worship. Draw me to you and free me to fulfill my purpose and your honor in holy worship.
—Amen.

w o r · s h i p

If you need wisdom—if you want to know what God wants you to do—ask him, and he will gladly tell you. He will not resent your asking. But when you ask him, be sure that you really expect him to answer.

James 1:5 – 6 NLT